DAN-74    DANTES SUBJECT STANDARDIZED TESTS (DSST)

*This is your*
*PASSBOOK for...*

# Introduction to World Religions

*Test Preparation Study Guide*
*Questions & Answers*

# COPYRIGHT NOTICE

This book is SOLELY intended for, is sold ONLY to, and its use is RESTRICTED to individual, bona fide applicants or candidates who qualify by virtue of having seriously filed applications for appropriate license, certificate, professional and/or promotional advancement, higher school matriculation, scholarship, or other legitimate requirements of education and/or governmental authorities.

This book is NOT intended for use, class instruction, tutoring, training, duplication, copying, reprinting, excerption, or adaptation, etc., by:

1) Other publishers
2) Proprietors and/or Instructors of "Coaching" and/or Preparatory Courses
3) Personnel and/or Training Divisions of commercial, industrial, and governmental organizations
4) Schools, colleges, or universities and/or their departments and staffs, including teachers and other personnel
5) Testing Agencies or Bureaus
6) Study groups which seek by the purchase of a single volume to copy and/or duplicate and/or adapt this material for use by the group as a whole without having purchased individual volumes for each of the members of the group
7) Et al.

Such persons would be in violation of appropriate Federal and State statutes.

PROVISION OF LICENSING AGREEMENTS – Recognized educational, commercial, industrial, and governmental institutions and organizations, and others legitimately engaged in educational pursuits, including training, testing, and measurement activities, may address request for a licensing agreement to the copyright owners, who will determine whether, and under what conditions, including fees and charges, the materials in this book may be used them.  In other words, a licensing facility exists for the legitimate use of the material in this book on other than an individual basis.  However, it is asseverated and affirmed here that the material in this book CANNOT be used without the receipt of the express permission of such a licensing agreement from the Publishers. Inquiries re licensing should be addressed to the company, attention rights and permissions department.

All rights reserved, including the right of reproduction in whole or in part, in any form or by any means, electronic or mechanical, including photocopying, recording, or by any information storage and retrieval system, without permission in writing from the Publisher.

Copyright © 2024 by
## National Learning Corporation

212 Michael Drive, Syosset, NY 11791
(516) 921-8888 • www.passbooks.com
E-mail: info@passbooks.com

PUBLISHED IN THE UNITED STATES OF AMERICA

# PASSBOOK® SERIES

THE *PASSBOOK® SERIES* has been created to prepare applicants and candidates for the ultimate academic battlefield – the examination room.

At some time in our lives, each and every one of us may be required to take an examination – for validation, matriculation, admission, qualification, registration, certification, or licensure.

Based on the assumption that every applicant or candidate has met the basic formal educational standards, has taken the required number of courses, and read the necessary texts, the *PASSBOOK® SERIES* furnishes the one special preparation which may assure passing with confidence, instead of failing with insecurity. Examination questions – together with answers – are furnished as the basic vehicle for study so that the mysteries of the examination and its compounding difficulties may be eliminated or diminished by a sure method.

This book is meant to help you pass your examination provided that you qualify and are serious in your objective.

The entire field is reviewed through the huge store of content information which is succinctly presented through a provocative and challenging approach – the question-and-answer method.

A climate of success is established by furnishing the correct answers at the end of each test.

You soon learn to recognize types of questions, forms of questions, and patterns of questioning. You may even begin to anticipate expected outcomes.

You perceive that many questions are repeated or adapted so that you can gain acute insights, which may enable you to score many sure points.

You learn how to confront new questions, or types of questions, and to attack them confidently and work out the correct answers.

You note objectives and emphases, and recognize pitfalls and dangers, so that you may make positive educational adjustments.

Moreover, you are kept fully informed in relation to new concepts, methods, practices, and directions in the field.

You discover that you are actually taking the examination all the time: you are preparing for the examination by "taking" an examination, not by reading extraneous and/or supererogatory textbooks.

In short, this PASSBOOK®, used directedly, should be an important factor in helping you to pass your test.

# NONTRADITIONAL EDUCATION

Students returning to school as adults bring more varied experience to their studies than do the teenagers who begin college shortly after graduating from high school. As a result, there are numerous programs for students with nontraditional learning curves. Hundreds of colleges and universities grant degrees to people who cannot attend classes at a regular campus or have already learned what the college is supposed to teach.

You can earn nontraditional education credits in many ways:
- Passing standardized exams
- Demonstrating knowledge gained through experience
- Completing campus-based coursework, and
- Taking courses off campus

Some methods of assessing learning for credit are objective, such as standardized tests. Others are more subjective, such as a review of life experiences.

With some help from four hypothetical characters – Alice, Vin, Lynette, and Jorge – this article describes nontraditional ways of earning educational credit. It begins by describing programs in which you can earn a high school diploma without spending 4 years in a classroom. The college picture is more complicated, so it is presented in two parts: one on gaining credit for what you know through course work or experience, and a second on college degree programs. The final section lists resources for locating more information.

## Earning High School Credit

People who were prevented from finishing high school as teenagers have several options if they want to do so as adults. Some major cities have back-to-school programs that allow adults to attend high school classes with current students. But the more practical alternatives for most adults are to take the General Educational Development (GED) tests or to earn a high school diploma by demonstrating their skills or taking correspondence classes.

Of course, these options do not match the experience of staying in high school and graduating with one's friends. But they are viable alternatives for adult learners committed to meeting and, often, continuing their educational goals.

### GED Program

Alice quit high school her sophomore year and took a job to help support herself, her younger brother, and their newly widowed mother. Now an adult, she wants to earn her high school diploma – and then go on to college. Because her job as head cook and her family responsibilities keep her busy during the day, she plans to get a high school equivalency diploma. She will study for, and take, the GED tests. Every year, about half a million adults earn their high school credentials this way. A GED diploma is accepted in lieu of a high school one by more than 90 percent of employers, colleges, and universities, so it is a good choice for someone like Alice.

The GED testing program is sponsored by the American Council on Education and State and local education departments. It consists of examinations in five subject areas: Writing, science, mathematics, social studies, and literature and the arts. The tests also measure skills such as analytical ability, problem solving, reading comprehension, and ability to understand and apply information. Most of the questions are multiple choice; the writing test includes an essay section on a topic of general interest.

Eligibility rules for taking the exams vary, but some states require that you must be at least 18. Tests are given in English, Spanish, and French. In addition to standard print, versions in large print, Braille, and audiocassette are also available. Total time allotted for the tests is 7 1/2 hours.

The GED tests are not easy. About one-fourth of those who complete the exams every year do not pass. Passing scores are established by administering the tests to a sample of graduating high school seniors. The minimum standard score is set so that about one-third of graduating seniors would not pass the tests if they took them.

Because of the difficulty of the tests, people need to prepare themselves to take them. Often, they start by taking the Official GED Practice Tests, usually available through a local adult education center. Centers are listed in your phone book's blue pages under "Adult Education," "Continuing Education," or "GED." Adult education centers also have information about GED preparation classes and self-study materials. Classes are generally arranged to accommodate adults' work schedules. National Learning Corporation publishes several study guides that aim to thoroughly prepare test-takers for the GED.

School districts, colleges, adult education centers, and community organizations have information about GED testing schedules and practice tests. For more information, contact them, your nearest GED testing center, or:

GED Testing Service
One Dupont Circle, NW, Suite 250
Washington, DC 20036-1163
1(800) 62-MY GED (626-9433)
(202) 939-9490

**Skills Demonstration**

Adults who have acquired high school level skills through experience might be eligible for the National External Diploma Program. This alternative to the GED does not involve any direct instruction. Instead, adults seeking a high school diploma must demonstrate mastery of 65 competencies in 8 general areas: Communication; computation; occupational preparedness; and self, social, consumer, scientific, and technological awareness.

Mastery is shown through the completion of the tasks. For example, a participant could prove competency in computation by measuring a room for carpeting, figuring out the amount of carpet needed, and computing the cost.

Before being accepted for the program, adults undergo an evaluation. Tests taken at one of the program's offices measure reading, writing, and mathematics abilities. A take-home segment includes a self-assessment of current skills, an individual skill evaluation, and an occupational interest and aptitude test.

Adults accepted for the program have weekly meetings with an assessor. At the meeting, the assessor reviews the participant's work from the previous week. If the task has not been completed properly, the assessor explains the mistake. Participants continue to correct their errors until they master each competency. A high school diploma is awarded upon proven mastery of all 65 competencies.

Fourteen States and the District of Columbia now offer the External Diploma Program. For more information, contact:
External Diploma Program
One Dupont Circle, NW, Suite 250
Washington, DC 20036-1193
(202) 939-9475

**Correspondence and Distance Study**
Vin dropped out of high school during his junior year because his family's frequent moves made it difficult for him to continue his studies. He promised himself at the time he dropped out that he would someday finish the courses needed for his diploma. For people like Vin, who prefer to earn a traditional diploma in a nontraditional way, there are about a dozen accredited courses of study for earning a high school diploma by correspondence, or distance study. The programs are either privately run, affiliated with a university, or administered by a State education department.

Distance study diploma programs have no residency requirements, allowing students to continue their studies from almost any location. Depending on the course of study, students need not be enrolled full time and usually have more flexible schedules for finishing their work. Selection of courses ranges from vo-tech to college prep, and some programs place different emphasis on the types of diplomas offered. University affiliated schools, for example, allow qualified students to take college courses along with their high school ones. Students can then apply the college credits toward a degree at that university or transfer them to another institution.

Taking courses by distance study is often more challenging and time consuming than attending classes, especially for adults who have other obligations. Success depends on each student's motivation. Students usually do reading assignments on their own. Written exercises, which they complete and send to an instructor for grading, supplement their reading material.

A list of some accredited high schools that offer diplomas by distance study is available free from the Distance Education and Training Council, formerly known as the National Home Study Council. Request the "DETC Directory of Accredited Institutions" from:
The Distance Education and Training Council
1601 18th Street, NW.
Washington, DC 20009-2529
(202) 234-5100

Some publications profiling nontraditional college programs include addresses and descriptions of several high school correspondence ones. See the Resources section at the end of this article for more information.

**Getting College Credit For What You Know**
Adults can receive college credit for prior coursework, by passing examinations, and documenting experiential learning. With help from a college advisor, nontraditional students should assess their skills, establish their educational goals, and determine the number of college credits they might be eligible for.

Even before you meet with a college advisor, you should collect all your school and training records. Then, make a list of all knowledge and abilities acquired through experience, no matter how irrelevant they seem to your chosen field. Next, determine your educational goals: What specific field do you wish to study? What kind of a degree do you want? Finally, determine how your past work fits into the field of study. Later on, you will evaluate educational programs to find one that's right for you.

People who have complex educational or experiential learning histories might want to have their learning evaluated by the Regents Credit Bank. The Credit Bank, operated by Regents College of the University of the State of New York, allows people to consolidate credits earned through college, experience, or other methods. Special assessments are available for Regents College enrollees whose knowledge in a specific field cannot be adequately evaluated by standardized exams. For more information, contact the Regents Credit Bank at:

>Regents College
>7 Columbia Circle
>Albany, NY 12203-5159
>(518) 464-8500

**Credit For Prior College Coursework**

When Lynette was in college during the 1970s, she attended several different schools and took a variety of courses. She did well in some classes and poorly in others. Now that she is a successful business owner and has more focus, Lynette thinks she should forget about her previous coursework and start from scratch. Instead, she should start from where she is.

Lynette should have all her transcripts sent to the colleges or universities of her choice and let an admissions officer determine which classes are applicable toward a degree. A few credits here and there may not seem like much, but they add up. Even if the subjects do not seem relevant to any major, they might be counted as elective credits toward a degree. And comparing the cost of transcripts with the cost of college courses, it makes sense to spend a few dollars per transcript for a chance to save hundreds, and perhaps thousands, of dollars in books and tuition.

Rules for transferring credits apply to all prior coursework at accredited colleges and universities, whether done on campus or off. Courses completed off campus, often called extended learning, include those available to students through independent study and correspondence. Many schools have extended learning programs; Brigham Young University, for example, offers more than 300 courses through its Department of Independent Study. One type of extended learning is distance learning, a form of correspondence study by technological means such as television, video and audio, CD-ROM, electronic mail, and computer tutorials. See the Resources section at the end of this article for more information about publications available from the National University Continuing Education Association.

Any previously earned college credits should be considered for transfer, no matter what the subject or the grade received. Many schools do not accept the transfer of courses graded below a C or ones taken more than a designated number of years ago. Some colleges and universities also have limits on the number of credits that can be transferred and applied toward a degree. But not all do. For example, Thomas Edison State College, New Jersey's State college for adults, accepts the transfer of all 120 hours of credit required for a baccalaureate degree – provided all the credits are transferred from regionally accredited schools, no more than 80 are at the junior college level, and the student's grades overall and in the field of study average out to C.

To assign credit for prior coursework, most schools require original transcripts. This means you must complete a form or send a written, signed request to have your transcripts released directly to a college or university. Once you have chosen the schools you want to apply to, contact the schools you attended before. Find out how much each transcript costs, and ask them to send your transcripts to the ones you are applying to. Write a letter that includes your name (and names used during attendance, if different) and dates of attendance, along with the names and addresses of the schools to which your transcripts should be sent. Include payment and mail to the registrar at the schools you have attended. The registrar's office will process your request and send an official transcript of your coursework to the colleges or universities you have designated.

**Credit For Noncollege Courses**

Colleges and universities are not the only ones that offer classes. Volunteer organizations and employers often provide formal training worth college credit. The American Council on Education has two programs that assess thousands of specific courses and make recommendations on the amount of college credit they are worth. Colleges and universities accept the recommendations or use them as guidelines.

One program evaluates educational courses sponsored by government agencies, business and industry, labor unions, and professional and voluntary organizations. It is the Program on Noncollegiate Sponsored Instruction (PONSI). Some of the training seminars Alice has participated in covered topics such as food preparation, kitchen safety, and nutrition. Although she has not yet earned her GED, Alice can earn college credit because of her completion of these formal job-training seminars. The number of credits each seminar is worth does not hinge on Alice's current eligibility for college enrollment.

The other program evaluates courses offered by the Army, Navy, Air Force, Marines, Coast Guard, and Department of Defense. It is the Military Evaluations Program. Jorge has never attended college, but the engineering technology classes he completed as part of his military training are worth college credit. And as an Army veteran, Jorge is eligible for a service that takes the evaluations one step further. The Army/American Council on Education Registry Transcript System (AARTS) will provide Jorge with an individualized transcript of American Council on Education credit recommendations for all courses he completed, the military occupational specialties (MOS's) he held, and examinations he passed while in the Army. All Army and National Guard enlisted personnel and veterans who enlisted after October 1981 are eligible for the transcript. Similar services are being considered by the Navy and Marine Corps.

To obtain a free transcript, see your Army Education Center for a 5454R transcript request form. Include your name, Social Security number, basic active service date, and complete address where you want the transcript sent. Mail your request to:
AARTS Operations Center
415 McPherson Ave.
Fort Leavenworth, KS 66027-1373

Recommendations for PONSI are published in *The National Guide to Educational Credit for Training Programs;* military program recommendations are in *The Guide to the Evaluation of Educational Experiences in the Armed Forces.* See the Resources section at the end of this article for more information about these publications.

Former military personnel who took a foreign language course through the Defense Language Institute may request course transcripts by sending their name, Social Security number, course title, duration of the course, and graduation date to:

Commandant, Defense Language Institute
Attn: ATFL-DAA-AR
Transcripts
Presidio of Monterey
Monterey, CA 93944-5006

Not all of Jorge's and Alice's courses have been assessed by the American Council on Education. Training courses that have no Council credit recommendation should still be assessed by an advisor at the schools they want to attend. Course descriptions, class notes, test scores, and other documentation may be helpful for comparing training courses to their college equivalents. An oral examination or other demonstration of competency might also be required.

There is no guarantee you will receive all the credits you are seeking – but you certainly won't if you make no attempt.

## Credit By Examination

Standardized tests are the best-known method of receiving college credit without taking courses. These exams are often taken by high school students seeking advanced placement for college, but they are also available to adult learners. Testing programs and colleges and universities offer exams in a number of subjects. Two U.S. Government institutes have foreign language exams for employees that also may be worth college credit.

It is important to understand that receiving a passing score on these exams does not mean you get college credit automatically. Each school determines which test results it will accept, minimum scores required, how scores are converted for credit, and the amount of credit, if any, to be assigned. Most colleges and universities accept the American Council on Education credit recommendations, published every other year in the 250-page *Guide to Educational Credit by Examination*. For more information, contact:

The American Council on Education
Credit by Examination Program
One Dupont Circle, Suite 250
Washington, DC 20036-1193
(202) 939-9434

### *Testing programs:*

You might know some of the five national testing programs by their acronyms or initials: CLEP, ACT PEP: RCE, DANTES, AP, and NOCTI. (The meanings of these initialisms are explained below.) There is some overlap among programs; for example, four of them have introductory accounting exams. Since you will not be awarded credit more than once for a specific subject, you should carefully evaluate each program for the subject exams you wish to take. And before taking an exam, make sure you will be awarded credit by the college or university you plan to attend.

CLEP (College-Level Examination Program), administered by the College Board, is the most widely accepted of the national testing programs; more than 2,800 accredited schools award credit for passing exam scores. Each test covers material taught in basic undergraduate courses. There are five general exams – English composition, humanities, college mathematics, natural sciences, and social sciences and history – and many subject exams. Most exams are entirely multiple-choice, but English composition exams may include an essay section. For more information, contact:

    CLEP
    P.O. Box 6600
    Princeton, NJ 08541-6600
    (609) 771-7865

ACT PEP: RCE (American College Testing Proficiency Exam Program: Regents College Examinations) tests are given in 38 subjects within arts and sciences, business, education, and nursing. Each exam is recommended for either lower- or upper-level credit. Exams contain either objective or extended response questions, and are graded according to a standard score, letter grade, or pass/fail. Fees vary, depending on the subject and type of exam. For more information or to request free study guides, contact:

    ACT PEP: Regents College Examinations
    P.O. Box 4014
    Iowa City, IA 52243
    (319) 337-1387
    (New York State residents must contact Regents College directly.)

DANTES (Defense Activity for Nontraditional Education Support) standardized tests are developed by the Educational Testing Service for the Department of Defense. Originally administered only to military personnel, the exams have been available to the public since 1983. About 50 subject tests cover business, mathematics, social science, physical science, humanities, foreign languages, and applied technology. Most of the tests consist entirely of multiple-choice questions. Schools determine their own administering fees and testing schedules. For more information or to request free study sheets, contact:

    DANTES Program Office
    Mail Stop 31-X
    Educational Testing Service
    Princeton, NJ 08541
    1(800) 257-9484

The AP (Advanced Placement) Program is a cooperative effort between secondary schools and colleges and universities. AP exams are developed each year by committees of college and high school faculty appointed by the College Board and assisted by consultants from the Educational Testing Service. Subjects include arts and languages, natural sciences, computer science, social sciences, history, and mathematics. Most tests are 2 or 3 hours long and include both multiple-choice and essay questions. AP courses are available to help students prepare for exams, which are offered in the spring. For more information about the Advanced Placement Program, contact:

    Advanced Placement Services
    P.O. Box 6671
    Princeton, NJ 08541-6671
    (609) 771-7300

NOCTI (National Occupational Competency Testing Institute) assessments are designed for people like Alice, who have vocational-technical skills that cannot be evaluated by other tests. NOCTI assesses competency at two levels: Student/job ready and teacher/experienced worker. Standardized evaluations are available for occupations such as auto-body repair, electronics, mechanical drafting, quantity food preparation, and upholstering. The tests consist of multiple-choice questions and a performance component. Other services include workshops, customized assessments, and pre-testing. For more information, contact:

NOCTI
500 N. Bronson Ave.
Ferris State University
Big Rapids, MI 49307
(616) 796-4699

### *Colleges and universities:*

Many colleges and universities have credit-by-exam programs, through which students earn credit by passing a comprehensive exam for a course offered by the institution. Among the most widely recognized are the programs at Ohio University, the University of North Carolina, Thomas Edison State College, and New York University.

Ohio University offers about 150 examinations for credit. In addition, you may sometimes arrange to take special examinations in non-laboratory courses offered at Ohio University. To take a test for credit, you must enroll in the course. If you plan to transfer the credit earned, you also need written permission from an official at your school. Books and study materials are available, for a cost, through the university. Exams must be taken within 6 months of the enrollment date; most last 3 hours. You may arrange to take the exam off campus if you do not live near the university.

Ohio University is on the quarter-hour system; most courses are worth 4 quarter hours, the equivalent of 3 semester hours. For more information, contact:

Independent Study
Tupper Hall 302
Ohio University
Athens, OH 45701-2979
1(800) 444-2910
(614) 593-2910

The University of North Carolina offers a credit-by-examination option for 140 independent study (correspondence) courses in foreign languages, humanities, social sciences, mathematics, business administration, education, electrical and computer engineering, health administration, and natural sciences. To take an exam, you must request and receive approval from both the course instructor and the independent studies department. Exams must be taken within six months of enrollment, and you may register for no more than two at a time. If you are not near the University's Chapel Hill campus, you may take your exam under supervision at an accredited college, university, community college, or technical institute. For more information, contact:

Independent Studies
CB #1020, The Friday Center
UNC-Chapel Hill
Chapel Hill, NC 27599-1020
1(800) 862-5669 / (919) 962-1134

The Thomas Edison College Examination Program offers more than 50 exams in liberal arts, business, and professional areas. Thomas Edison State College administers tests twice a month in Trenton, New Jersey; however, students may arrange to take their tests with a proctor at any accredited American college or university or U.S. military base. Most of the tests are multiple choice; some also include short answer or essay questions. Time limits range from 90 minutes to 4 hours, depending on the exam. For more information, contact:

Thomas Edison State College
TECEP, Office of Testing and Assessment
101 W. State Street
Trenton, NJ 08608-1176
(609) 633-2844

New York University's Foreign Language Program offers proficiency exams in more than 40 languages, from Albanian to Yiddish. Two exams are available in each language: The 12-point test is equivalent to 4 undergraduate semesters, and the 16-point exam may lead to upper level credit. The tests are given at the university's Foreign Language Department throughout the year.

Proof of foreign language proficiency does not guarantee college credit. Some colleges and universities accept transcripts only for languages commonly taught, such as French and Spanish. Nontraditional programs are more likely than traditional ones to grant credit for proficiency in other languages.

For an informational brochure and registration form for NYU's foreign language proficiency exams, contact:

New York University
Foreign Language Department
48 Cooper Square, Room 107
New York, NY 10003
(212) 998-7030

***Government institutes:***

The Defense Language Institute and Foreign Service Institute administer foreign language proficiency exams for personnel stationed abroad. Usually, the tests are given at the end of intensive language courses or upon completion of service overseas. But some people -- like Jorge, who knows Spanish -- speak another language fluently and may be allowed to take a proficiency exam in that language before completing their tour of duty. Contact one of the offices listed below to obtain transcripts of those scores. Proof of proficiency does not guarantee college credit, however, as discussed above.

To request score reports from the Defense Language Institute for Defense Language Proficiency Tests, send your name, Social Security number, language for which you were tested, and, most importantly, when and where you took the exam to:

Commandant, Defense Language Institute
Attn: ATFL-ES-T
DLPT Score Report Request
Presidio of Monterey
Monterey, CA 93944-5006

To request transcripts of scores for Foreign Service Institute exams, send your name, Social Security number, language for which you were tested, and dates or year of exams to:

Foreign Service Institute
Arlington Hall
4020 Arlington Boulevard
Rosslyn, VA 22204-1500
Attn: Testing Office (Send your request to the attention of the testing office of the foreign language in which you were tested)

**Credit For Experience**

Experiential learning credit may be given for knowledge gained through job responsibilities, personal hobbies, volunteer opportunities, homemaking, and other experiences. Colleges and universities base credit awards on the knowledge you have attained, not for the experience alone. In addition, the knowledge must be college level; not just any learning will do. Throwing horseshoes as a hobby is not likely to be worth college credit. But if you've done research on how and where the sport originated, visited blacksmiths, organized tournaments, and written a column for a trade journal – well, that's a horseshoe of a different color.

Adults attempting to get credit for their experience should be forewarned: Having your experience evaluated for college credit is time-consuming, tedious work – not an easy shortcut for people who want quick-fix college credits. And not all experience, no matter how valuable, is the equivalent of college courses.

Requesting college credit for your experiential learning can be tricky. You should get assistance from a credit evaluations officer at the school you plan to attend, but you should also have a general idea of what your knowledge is worth. A common method for converting knowledge into credit is to use a college catalog. Find course titles and descriptions that match what you have learned through experience, and request the number of credits offered for those courses.

Once you know what credit to ask for, you must usually present your case in writing to officials at the college you plan to attend. The most common form of presenting experiential learning for credit is the portfolio. A portfolio is a written record of your knowledge along with a request for equivalent college credit. It includes an identification and description of the knowledge for which you are requesting credit, an explanatory essay of how the knowledge was gained and how it fits into your educational plans, documentation that you have acquired such knowledge, and a request for college credit. Required elements of a portfolio vary by schools but generally follow those guidelines.

In identifying knowledge you have gained, be specific about exactly what you have learned. For example, it is not enough for Lynette to say she runs a business. She must identify the knowledge she has gained from running it, such as personnel management, tax law, marketing strategy, and inventory review. She must also include brief descriptions about her knowledge of each to support her claims of having those skills.

The essay gives you a chance to relay something about who you are. It should address your educational goals, include relevant autobiographical details, and be well organized, neat, and convey confidence. In his essay, Jorge might first state his goal of becoming an engineer. Then he would explain why he joined the Army, where he got hands-on training and experience in developing and servicing electronic equipment.

This, he would say, led to his hobby of creating remote-controlled model cars, of which he has built 20. His conclusion would highlight his accomplishments and tie them to his desire to become an electronic engineer.

Documentation is evidence that you've learned what you claim to have learned. You can show proof of knowledge in a variety of ways, including audio or video recordings, letters from current or former employers describing your specific duties and job performance, blueprints, photographs or artwork, and transcripts of certifying exams for professional licenses and certification – such as Alice's certification from the American Culinary Federation. Although documentation can take many forms, written proof alone is not always enough. If it is impossible to document your knowledge in writing, find out if your experiential learning can be assessed through supplemental oral exams by a faculty expert.

## Earning a College Degree

Nontraditional students often have work, family, and financial obligations that prevent them from quitting their jobs to attend school full time. Can they still meet their educational goals? Yes.

More than 150 accredited colleges and universities have nontraditional bachelor's degree programs that require students to spend little or no time on campus; over 300 others have nontraditional campus-based degree programs. Some of those schools, as well as most junior and community colleges, offer associate's degrees nontraditionally. Each school with a nontraditional course of study determines its own rules for awarding credit for prior coursework, exams, or experience, as discussed previously. Most have charges on top of tuition for providing these special services.

Several publications profile nontraditional degree programs; see the Resources section at the end of this article for more information. To determine which school best fits your academic profile and educational goals, first list your criteria. Then, evaluate nontraditional programs based on their accreditation, features, residency requirements, and expenses. Once you have chosen several schools to explore further, write to them for more information. Detailed explanations of school policies should help you decide which ones you want to apply to.

Get beyond the printed word – especially the glowing words each school writes about itself. Check out the schools you are considering with higher education authorities, alumni, employers, family members, and friends. If possible, visit the campus to talk to students and instructors and sit in on a few classes, even if you will be completing most or all of your work off campus. Ask school officials questions about such things as enrollment numbers, graduation rate, faculty qualifications, and confusing details about the application process or academic policies. After you have thoroughly investigated each prospective college or university, you can make an informed decision about which is right for you.

### Accreditation

Accreditation is a process colleges and universities submit to voluntarily for getting their credentials. An accredited school has been investigated and visited by teams of observers and has periodic inspections by a private accrediting agency. The initial review can take two years or more.

Regional agencies accredit entire schools, and professional agencies accredit either specialized schools or departments within schools. Although there are no national accrediting standards, not just any accreditation will do. Countless "accreditation associations" have been invented by schools, many of which have no academic programs and sell phony degrees, to accredit themselves. But 6 regional and about 80 professional accrediting associations in the United States are recognized by the U.S. Department of Education or the Commission on Recognition of Postsecondary Accreditation. When checking accreditation, these are the names to look for. For more information about accreditation and accrediting agencies, contact:

> Institutional Participation Oversight Service Accreditation and State Liaison Division
> U.S. Department of Education
> ROB 3, Room 3915
> 600 Independence Ave., SW
> Washington, DC 20202-5244
> (202) 708-7417

Because accreditation is not mandatory, lack of accreditation does not necessarily mean a school or program is bad. Some schools choose not to apply for accreditation, are in the process of applying, or have educational methods too unconventional for an accrediting association's standards. For the nontraditional student, however, earning a degree from a college or university with recognized accreditation is an especially important consideration. Although nontraditional education is becoming more widely accepted, it is not yet mainstream. Employers skeptical of a degree earned in a nontraditional manner are likely to be even less accepting of one from an unaccredited school.

**Program Features**

Because nontraditional students have diverse educational objectives, nontraditional schools are diverse in what they offer. Some programs are geared toward helping students organize their scattered educational credits to get a degree as quickly as possible. Others cater to those who may have specific credits or experience but need assistance in completing requirements. Whatever your educational profile, you should look for a program that works with you in obtaining your educational goals.

A few nontraditional programs have special admissions policies for adult learners like Alice, who plan to earn their GEDs but want to enroll in college in the meantime. Other features of nontraditional programs include individualized learning agreements, intensive academic counseling, cooperative learning and internship placement, and waiver of some prerequisites or other requirements – as well as college credit for prior coursework, examinations, and experiential learning, all discussed previously.

Lynette, whose primary goal is to finish her degree, wants to earn maximum credits for her business experience. She will look for programs that do not limit the number of credits awarded for equivalency exams and experiential learning. And since well-documented proof of knowledge is essential for earning experiential learning credits, Lynette should make sure the program she chooses provides assistance to students submitting a portfolio.

Jorge, on the other hand, has more credits than he needs in certain areas and is willing to forego some. To become an engineer, he must have a bachelor's degree; but because he is accustomed to hands-on learning, Jorge is interested in getting experience as he gains more technical skills. He will concentrate on finding schools with strong cooperative education, supervised fieldwork, or internship programs.

## Residency Requirements

Programs are sometimes deemed nontraditional because of their residency requirements. Many people think of residency for colleges and universities in terms of tuition, with in-state students paying less than out-of-state ones. Residency also may refer to where a student lives, either on or off campus, while attending school.

But in nontraditional education, residency usually refers to how much time students must spend on campus, regardless of whether they attend classes there. In some nontraditional programs, students need not ever step foot on campus. Others require only a very short residency, such as one day or a few weeks. Many schools have standard residency requirements of several semesters but schedule classes for evenings or weekends to accommodate working adults.

Lynette, who previously took courses by independent study, prefers to earn credits by distance study. She will focus on schools that have no residency requirement. Several colleges and universities have nonresident degree completion programs for adults with some college credit. Under the direction of a faculty advisor, students devise a plan for earning their remaining credits. Methods for earning credits include independent study, distance learning, seminars, supervised fieldwork, and group study at arranged sites. Students may have to earn a certain number of credits through the degree-granting institution. But many programs allow students to take courses at accredited schools of their choice for transfer toward their degree.

Alice wants to attend lectures but has an unpredictable schedule. Her best course of action will be to seek out short residency programs that require students to attend seminars once or twice a semester. She can take courses that are televised and videotape them to watch when her schedule permits, with the seminars helping to ensure that she properly completes her coursework. Many colleges and universities with short residency requirements also permit students to earn some credits elsewhere, by whatever means the student chooses.

Some fields of study require classroom instruction. As Jorge will discover, few colleges and universities allow students to earn a bachelor's degree in engineering entirely through independent study. Nontraditional residency programs are designed to accommodate adults' daytime work schedules. Jorge should look for programs offering evening, weekend, summer, and accelerated courses.

## Tuition and Other Expenses

The final decisions about which schools Alice, Jorge, and Lynette attend may hinge in large part on a single issue: Cost. And rising tuition is only part of the equation. Beginning with application fees and continuing through graduation fees, college expenses add up.

Traditional and nontraditional students have some expenses in common, such as the cost of books and other materials. Tuition might even be the same for some courses, especially for colleges and universities offering standard ones at unusual times. But for nontraditional programs, students may also pay fees for services such as credit or transcript review, evaluation, advisement, and portfolio assessment.

Students are also responsible for postage and handling or setup expenses for independent study courses, as well as for all examination and transcript fees for transferring credits. Usually, the more nontraditional the program, the more detailed the fees. Some schools charge a yearly enrollment fee rather than tuition for degree completion candidates who want their files to remain active.

Although tuition and fees might seem expensive, most educators tell you not to let money come between you and your educational goals. Talk to someone in the financial aid department of the school you plan to attend or check your library for publications about financial aid sources. The U.S. Department of Education publishes a guide to Federal aid programs such as Pell Grants, student loans, and work-study. To order the free 74-page booklet, *The Student Guide: Financial Aid from the U.S. Department of Education,* contact:

    Federal Student Aid Information Center
    P.O. Box 84
    Washington, DC 20044
    1 (800) 4FED-AID (433-3243)

**Resources**

Information on how to earn a high school diploma or college degree without following the usual routes is available from several organizations and in numerous publications. Information on nontraditional graduate degree programs, available for master's through doctoral level, though not discussed in this article, can usually be obtained from the same resources that detail bachelor's degree programs.

National Learning Corporation publishes study guides for all of these exams, for both general examinations and tests in specific subject areas. To order study guides, or to browse their catalog featuring more than 5,000 titles, visit NLC online at www.passbooks.com, or contact them by phone at (800) 632-8888.

**Organizations**

Adult learners should always contact their local school system, community college, or university to learn about programs that are readily available. The following national organizations can also supply information:

    American Council on Education
    One Dupont Circle
    Washington, DC 20036-1193
    (202) 939-9300

Within the American Council on Education, the Center for Adult Learning and Educational Credentials administers the National External Diploma Program, the GED Program, the Program on Noncollegiate Sponsored Instruction, the Credit by Examination Program, and the Military Evaluations Program.

# DANTES Subject Standardized Tests

## INTRODUCTION

The DANTES (Defense Activity for Non-Traditional Education Support) subject standardized tests are comprehensive college and graduate level examinations given by the Armed Forces, colleges and graduate schools as end-of-subject course evaluation final examinations or to obtain college equivalency credits in the various subject areas tested.

The DANTES Examination Program enables students to obtain college credit for what they have learned on the job, through self-study, personal interest, correspondence courses or by any other means. It is used by colleges and universities to award college credit to students who demonstrate that they know as much as students completing an equivalent college course. It is a cost-efficient, time-saving way for students to use their knowledge to accomplish their educational goals.

Most schools accept the American Council on Education (ACE) recommendations for the minimum score required and the amount of credit awarded, but not all schools do. Be sure to check the policy regarding the score level required for credit and the number of credits to be awarded.

Not all tests are accepted by all institutions. Even when a test is accepted by an institution, it may not be acceptable for every program at that institution. Before considering testing, ascertain the acceptability of a specific test for a particular course.

Colleges and universities that administer DANTES tests may administer them to any applicant – or they may administer the tests only to students registered at their institution. Decisions about who will be allowed to test are made by the school. Students should contact the test center to determine current policies and schedules for DANTES testing.

Colleges and universities authorized to administer DANTES tests usually do so throughout the calendar year. Each school sets its own fee for test administration and establishes its own testing schedule. Contact the representative at the administering school directly to make arrangements for testing.

# Checklist
## For Students

✓ Visit **www.getcollegecredit.com** to obtain a list of tests, fact sheets, test preparation materials, participating colleges and universities, and much more.

✓ Contact your school advisor to confirm that the DSST you selected will fit into your curriculum.

✓ Consult the ***DSST Candidate Information Bulletin*** for answers to specific questions.

✓ Contact the test site to schedule your test.

✓ Prepare for your examination by using the fact sheet as a guide.

✓ Take the test.

*If you would like a score report sent to your college or university, it is a good idea to bring the four-digit code with you. You must write the DSST Test Center Code for that institution on your answer sheet at the time of testing. DSST Test Center Codes are noted in the DSST Participating Colleges and Universities listing on the Web site.*

*If you prefer to send a score report to an institution at a later date, there is a transcript fee of $20 for each transcript ordered.*

Thomson Prometric
DSST Program
2000 Lenox Drive, Third Floor
Lawrenceville, NJ 08648

Toll-free: 877-471-9860
609-895-5011

E-mail: pnj-dsst@thomson.com

# MAKING A COLLEGE DEGREE WITHIN YOUR REACH

Today, there are many educational alternatives to the classroom—you can learn from your job, your reading, your independent study, and special interests you pursue. You may already have learned the subject matter covered by some college-level courses.

The DSST Program is a nationally recognized testing program that gives you the opportunity to receive college credit for learning acquired outside the traditional college classroom. Colleges and universities throughout the United States administer the program, developed by Thomson Prometric, year-round. Annually, over 90,000 DSSTs are administered to individuals who are interested in continuing their education. Take advantage of the DSST testing program; it speeds the educational process and provides the flexibility adults need, making earning a degree more feasible.

Since requirements differ from college to college, please check with the credit-awarding institution before taking a DSST. More than 1,800 colleges and universities currently award credit for DSSTs, and the number is growing every day. You can choose from 37 test titles in the areas of Social Science, Business, Mathematics, Applied Technology, Humanities, and Physical Science. A brief description of each examination is found on the pages that follow.

## Reach Your Career Goals Through DSSTs

Use DSSTs to help you earn your degree, get a promotion, or simply demonstrate that you have college-level knowledge in subjects relevant to your work.

### *Save Time...*

You don't have to sit through classes when you have previously acquired the knowledge or experience for most of what is being taught and can learn the rest yourself. You might be able to bypass introductory-level courses in subject areas you already know.

### *Save Money...*

DSSTs save you money because the classes you bypass by earning credit through the DSST Program are classes you won't have to pay for on your way to earning your degree. You can use the money instead to take more advanced courses that can be more challenging and rewarding.

## Improve Your Chances for Admission to College

Each college has its own admission policies; however, having passing scores for DSSTs on your transcript can provide strong evidence of how well you can perform at the college level.

## Gain Confidence Performing at a College Level

Many adults returning to college find that lack of confidence is often the greatest hurdle to overcome. Passing a DSST demonstrates your ability to perform on a college level.

**Make Up for Courses You May Have Missed**

You may be ready to graduate from college and find that you are a few credits short of earning your degree. By using semester breaks, vacation time, or leisure time to study independently, you can prepare to take one or more DSSTs, fulfill your academic requirements, and graduate on time.

**If You Cannot Attend Regularly Scheduled Classes...**

If your lifestyle or responsibilities prevent you from attending regularly scheduled classes, you can earn your college degree from a college offering an external degree program. The DSST Program allows you to earn your degree by study and experience outside the traditional classroom.

Many colleges and universities offer external degree or distance learning programs. For additional information, contact the college you plan to attend or:

Center for Lifelong Learning
American Council on Education
One DuPont Circle NW, Suite 250
Washington, DC 20036
202-939-9475
www.acenet.edu
(Select "Center for Lifelong Learning" under "Programs & Services"
for more information)

**Fact Sheets**

For each test, there is a Fact Sheet that outlines the topics covered by each test and includes a list of sample questions, a list of recommended references of books that would be useful for review, and the number of credits awarded for a passing score as recommended by the American Council on Education (ACE). *Please note that some schools require scores that are higher than the minimum ACE-recommended passing score.* It is suggested that you check with your college or university to determine what score they require in order to earn credit. You can obtain Fact Sheets by:
- Downloading them from www.getcollegecredit.com
- E-mailing a request to pnj-dsst@thomson.com
- Completing a Candidate Publications Order Form

**DSST Online Practice Tests**

DSST online practice tests contain items that reflect a *partial range of difficulty* identified in the Content Outline section on each Fact Sheet. There is an online DSST Practice Test in the following categories:
- Mathematics
- Social Science
- Business
- Physical Science
- Applied Technology
- Humanities

Although the online DSST Practice Test questions do not indicate the full range of difficulty you would find in an actual DSST test, they will help you assess your knowledge level. Each online DSST Practice Test can be purchased by visiting www.getcollegecredit.com and clicking on DSST Practice Exams.

# TAKING DSST EXAMINATIONS

## Earning College Credit for DSST Examinations

To find out if the college of your choice awards credit for passing DSST scores, contact the admissions office or counseling and testing office. The college can also provide information on the scores required for awarding credit, the number of credit hours awarded, and any courses that can be bypassed with satisfactory scores.

<u>*It is important that you contact the institution of your choice as early as possible since credit-awarding policies differ among colleges and universities.*</u>

## Where to Take DSSTs

DSSTs are administered at colleges and universities nationwide. Each location determines the frequency and scheduling of test administrations. To obtain the most current list of participating DSST colleges and universities:
- Visit and download the information from www.getcollegecredit.com
- E-mail pnj-dsst@thomson.com

## Scheduling Your Examination

*Please be aware that some colleges and universities provide DSST testing services to enrolled students only.* After you have selected a college or university that administers DSSTs, you will need to contact them to schedule your test date.

The fee to take a DSST is $60 per test. This fee entitles you to two score reports after the test is scored. One will be sent directly to you and the other will be sent to the college or university that you designate on your answer sheet. You may pay the test fee with a certified check or U.S. money order made payable to Thomson Prometric or you may charge the test fee to your Visa, MasterCard or American Express credit card. Note: The credit card statement will reflect a charge from Thomson Prometric for all DSST examinations. *(Declined credit card charges will be assessed an additional $25 processing fee.)*

In addition, the test site may also require a test administration fee for each examination, to be paid directly to the institution. Contact the test site to determine its administration fee and payment policy.

## Other Testing Arrangements

If you are unable to find a participating DSST college or university in your area, you may want to contact the testing office of a local accredited college or university to determine whether a representative from that office will agree to administer the test(s) for you.

The school's representative should then contact the DSST Program at 866-794-3497 to arrange for this administration. If you are unable to locate a test site, contact Thomson Prometric for assistance at pnj-dsst@thomson.com or 866-794-3497.

## Testing Accommodations for Students with Disabilities

Thomson Prometric is committed to serving test takers with disabilities by providing services and reasonable testing accommodations as set forth in the provisions of the *Americans with Disabilities Act* (ADA). If you have a disability, as prescribed by the ADA, and require special testing services or arrangements, please contact the test administrator at the test site. You will be asked to submit to the test administrator documentation of your disability and your request for special accommodations. The test administrator will then forward your documentation along with your request for testing accommodations to Thomson Prometric for approval.

Please submit your request as far in advance of your test date as possible so that the necessary accommodations can be made. Only test takers with documented disabilities are eligible for special accommodations.

**On the Day of the Examination**

It is important to review this information and to have the correct identification present on the day of the examination:
- Arrive on time as a courtesy to the test administrator.
- Bring a valid form of government-issued identification that includes a current photo and your signature (acceptable documents include a driver's license, passport, state-issued identification card or military identification). *Anyone who fails to present valid identification will not be allowed to test.*
- Bring several No. 2 (soft-lead) sharpened pencils with good erasers, a watch, and a black pen if you will be writing an essay.
- Do not bring books or papers.
- Do not bring an alarm watch that beeps, a telephone, or a phone beeper into the testing room.
- The use of nonprogrammable calculators, slide rules, scratch paper and/or other materials is permitted for some of the tests.

## DSST SCORING POLICIES

Your DSST examination scores are reported only to you, unless you request that they be sent elsewhere. If you want your scores sent to your college, you must provide the correct DSST code number of the school on your answer sheet at the time you take the test. See the *DSST Directory of Colleges and Universities* on the Web site www.getcollegecredit.com.

If your institution is not listed, contact Thomson Prometric at 866-794-3497 to establish a code number. (Some schools may require a student to be enrolled prior to receiving a score report.)

**Receiving Your Score Report**

Allow approximately four weeks after testing to receive your score report.

Calling DSST Customer Service before the required four-week score processing time has elapsed will not expedite the processing of your scores. Due to privacy and security requirements, scores will not be reported to students over the telephone under any circumstance.

**Scoring of Principles of Public Speaking Speeches**

The speech portion of the *Principles of Public Speaking* examination will be sent to speech raters who are faculty members at accredited colleges that currently teach or have previously taught the course. Scores for the *Principles of Public Speaking* examination are available six to eight weeks from receipt by Thomson Prometric. If you take the *Principles of Public Speaking* examination and fail (either the objective, speech portion, or both), you must follow the retesting policy waiting period of six months (180 days) before retaking the entire exam.

## Essays

The essays for *Ethics in America* and *Technical Writing* are optional and thus are not scored by raters. The essays are forwarded to the college or university that you designate, along with your score report, for their use in determining the award of credit. Before taking the *Ethics in America* or *Technical Writing* examinations, check with your college or university to determine whether the essay is required.

**NOTE:** *Principles of Public Speaking* speech topic cassette tapes and essays are kept on file at Thomson Prometric for one year from the date of administration.

## How to Get Transcripts

There is a $20 fee for each transcript you request. Payment must be in the form of a certified check, U.S. money order payable to Thomson Prometric, or credit card. Personal checks and debit cards are NOT an acceptable method of payment. One transcript may include scores for one or more examinations taken. To request a transcript, download the Transcript Order Form from www.getcollegecredit.com.

# DESCRIPTION OF THE DSST EXAMINATIONS

## Mathematics

- **Fundamentals of College Algebra** covers mathematical concepts such as fundamental algebraic operations; linear, absolute value; quadratic equations, inequalities, radials, exponents and logarithms, factoring polynomials and graphing. The use of a nonprogrammable, handheld calculator is permitted.

- **Principles of Statistics** tests the understanding of the various topics of statistics, both qualitatively and quantitatively, and the ability to apply statistical methods to solve a variety of problems. The topics included in this test are descriptive statistics; correlation and regression; probability; chance models and sampling and tests of significance. The use of a nonprogrammable, handheld calculator is permitted.

## Social Science

- **Art of the Western World** deals with the history of art during the following periods: classical; Romanesque and Gothic; early Renaissance; high Renaissance, Baroque; rococo; neoclassicism and romanticism; realism, impressionism and post-impressionism; early twentieth century; and post-World War II.

- **Western Europe Since 1945** tests the knowledge of basic facts and terms and the understanding of concepts and principles related to the areas of the historical background of the aftermath of the Second World War and rebuilding of Europe; national political systems; issues and policies in Western European societies; European institutions and processes; and Europe's relations with the rest of the world.

- **An Introduction to the Modern Middle East** emphasizes core knowledge (including geography, Judaism, Christianity, Islam, ethnicity); nineteenth-century European impact; twentieth-century Western influences; World Wars I and II; new nations; social and cultural changes (1900-1960) and the Middle East from 1960 to present.

- **Human/Cultural Geography** includes the Earth and basic facts (coordinate systems, maps, physiography, atmosphere, soils and vegetation, water); culture and environment, spatial processes (social processes, modern economic systems, settlement patterns, political geography); and regional geography.

- **Rise and Fall of the Soviet Union** covers Russia under the Old Regime; the Revolutionary Period; New Economic Policy; Pre-war Stalinism; The Second World War; Post-war Stalinism; The Khrushchev Years; The Brezhnev Era; and reform and collapse.

- **A History of the Vietnam War** covers the history of the roots of the Vietnam War; the First Vietnam War (1946-1954); pre-war developments (1954-1963); American involvement in the Vietnam War; Tet (1968); Vietnamizing the War (1968-1973); Cambodia and Laos; peace; legacies and lessons.

- **The Civil War and Reconstruction** covers the Civil War from presecession (1861) through Reconstruction. It includes causes of the war; secession; Fort Sumter; the war in the east and in the west; major battles; the political situation; assassination of Lincoln; end of the Confederacy; and Reconstruction.

- **Foundations of Education** includes topics such as contemporary issues in education; past and current influences on education (philosophies, democratic ideals, social/economic influences); and the interrelationships between contemporary issues and influences.

- **Life-span Developmental Psychology** covers models and theories; methods of study; ethical issues; biological development; perception, learning and memory; cognition and language; social, emotional, and personality development; social behaviors, family life cycle, extrafamilial settings; singlehood and cohabitation; occupational development and retirement; adjustment to life stresses; and bereavement and loss.

- **Drug and Alcohol Abuse** includes such topics as drug use in society; classification of drugs; pharmacological principles; alcohol (types, effects of, alcoholism); general principles and use of sedative hypnotics, narcotic analgesics, stimulants, and hallucinogens; other drugs (inhalants, steroids); and prevention/treatment.

- **General Anthropology** deals with anthropology as a discipline; theoretical perspectives; physical anthropology; archaeology; social organization; economic organization; political organization; religion; and modernization and application of anthropology.

- **Introduction to Law Enforcement** includes topics such as history and professional movement of law enforcement; overview of the U.S. criminal justice system; police systems in the U.S.; police organization, management, and issues; and U.S. law and precedents.

- **Criminal Justice** deals with criminal behavior (crime in the U.S., theories of crime, types of crime); the criminal justice system (historical origins, legal foundations, due process); police; the court system (history and organization, adult court system, juvenile court, pre-trial and post-trial processes); and corrections.

- **Fundamentals of Counseling** covers historical development (significant influences and people); counselor roles and functions; the counseling relationship; and theoretical approaches to counseling.

**Business**
- **Principles of Finance** deals with financial statements and planning; time value of money; working capital management; valuation and characteristics; capital budgeting; cost of capital; risk and return; and international financial management. The use of a nonprogrammable, handheld calculator is permitted.

- **Principles of Financial Accounting** includes topics such as general concepts and principles, accounting cycle and classification; transaction analysis; accruals and deferrals; cash and internal control; current accounts; long- and short-term liabilities; capital stock; and financial statements. The use of a nonprogrammable, handheld calculator is permitted.

- **Human Resource Management** covers general employment issues; job analysis; training and development; performance appraisals; compensation issues; security issues; personnel legislation and regulation; labor relations and current issues; an overview of the Human Resource Management Field; Human Resource Planning; Staffing; training and development; compensation issues; safety and health; employee rights and discipline; employment law; labor relations and current issues and trends.

- **Organizational Behavior** deals with the study of organizational behavior (scientific approaches, research designs, data collection methods); individual processes and characteristics; interpersonal and group processes and characteristics; organizational processes and characteristics; and change and development processes.

- **Principles of Supervision** deals with the roles and responsibilities of the supervisor; management functions (planning, organization and staffing, directing at the supervisory level); and other topics (legal issues, stress management, union environments, quality concerns).

- **Business Law II** covers topics such as sales of goods; debtor and creditor relations; business organizations; property; and commercial paper.

- **Introduction to Computing** includes topics such as history and technological generations; hardware/software; applications to information technology; program development; data management; communications and connectivity; and computing and society. The use of a nonprogrammable, handheld calculator is permitted.

- **Management Information Systems** covers systems theory, analysis and design of systems, hardware and software; database management; telecommunications; management of the MIS functional area and informational support.

- **Introduction to Business** deals with economic issues affecting business; international business; government and business; forms of business ownership; small business, entrepreneurship and franchise; management process; human resource management; production and operations; marketing management; financial management; risk management and insurance; and management and information systems.

- **Money and Banking** covers the role and kinds of money; commercial banks and other financial intermediaries; central banking and the Federal Reserve system; money and macroeconomics activity; monetary policy in the U.S.; and the international monetary system.

- **Personal Finance** includes topics such as financial goals and values; budgeting; credit and debt; major purchases; taxes; insurance; investments; and retirement and estate planning. The use of auxiliary materials, such as calculators and slide rules, is NOT permitted.

- **Business Mathematics** deals with basic operations with integers, fractions, and decimals; round numbers; ratios; averages; business graphs; simple interest; compound interest and annuities; net pay and deductions; discounts and markups; depreciation and net worth; corporate securities; distribution of ownership; and stock and asset turnover.

**Physical Science**
• **Astronomy** covers the history of astronomy, celestial mechanics; celestial systems; astronomical instruments; the solar system; nature and evolution; the galaxy; the universe; determining astronomical distances; and life in the universe.

• **Here's to Your Health** covers mental health and behavior; human development and relationships; substance abuse; fitness and nutrition; risk factors, disease, and disease prevention; and safety, consumer awareness, and environmental concerns.

• **Environment and Humanity** deals with topics such as ecological concepts (ecosystems, global ecology, food chains and webs); environmental impacts; environmental management and conservation; and political processes and the future.

• **Principles of Physical Science I** includes physics: Newton's Laws of Motion; energy and momentum; thermodynamics; wave and optics; electricity and magnetism; chemistry: properties of matter; atomic theory and structure; and chemical reactions.

• **Physical Geology** covers Earth materials; igneous, sedimentary, and metamorphic rocks; surface processes (weathering, groundwater, glaciers, oceanic systems, deserts and winds, hydrologic cycle); internal Earth processes; and applications (mineral and energy resources, environmental geology).

**Applied Technology**
• **Technical Writing** covers topics such as theory and practice of technical writing; purpose, content, and organizational patterns of common types of technical documents; elements of various technical reports; and technical editing. Students have the option to write a short essay on one of the technical topics provided. Thomson Prometric will not score the essay; however, for determining the award of credit, a copy of the essay will be forwarded to the college or university you've designated along with the score report or transcript.

**Humanities**
• **Ethics in America** deals with ethical traditions (Greek views, Biblical traditions, moral law, consequential ethics, feminist ethics); ethical analysis of issues arising in interpersonal and personal-societal relationships and in professional and occupational roles; and relationships between ethical traditions and the ethical analysis of situations. Students have the option to write an essay to analyze a morally problematic situation in terms of issues relevant to a decision and arguments for alternative positions. Thomson Prometric will not score the essay; however, for determining the award of credit, a copy of the essay will be forwarded to the college or university you've designated along with the score report or transcript.

• **Introduction to World Religions** covers topics such as dimensions and approaches to religion; primal religions; Hinduism; Buddhism; Confucianism; Taoism; Judaism; Christianity; and Islam.

• **Principles of Public Speaking** consists of two parts: Part One consists of multiple-choice questions covering considerations of Principles of Public Speaking; audience analysis; purposes of speeches; structure/organization; content/supporting materials; research; language and style; delivery; communication apprehension; listening and feedback; and criticism and evaluation. Part Two requires the student to record an impromptu persuasive speech that will be scored.

# FREQUENTLY ASKED QUESTIONS ABOUT DSSTs

*In order to pass the test, must I study from one of the recommended references?*

The recommended references are a listing of books that were being used as textbooks in college courses of the same or similar title at the time the test was developed. Appropriate textbooks for study are not limited to those listed in the fact sheet. If you wish to obtain study resources to prepare for the examination, you may reference either the current edition of the listed titles or textbooks currently used at a local college or university for the same class title. It is recommended that you reference more than one textbook on the topics outlined in the fact sheet. You should begin by checking textbook content against the content outline included on the front page of the DSST fact sheet before selecting textbooks that cover the text content from which to study. Textbooks may be found at the campus bookstore of a local college or university offering a course on the subject.

*Is there a penalty for guessing on the tests?*

There is no penalty for guessing on DSSTs, so you should mark an answer for each question.

*How much time will I have to complete the test?*

Many DSSTs can be completed within 90 minutes; however, additional time can be allowed if necessary.

*What should I do if I find a test question irregularity?*

Continue testing and then report the irregularity to the test administrator after the test. This may be done by asking that the test administrator note the irregularity on the Supervisor's Irregularity Report or you can write to Thomson Prometric, DSST Program, 2000 Lenox Drive, Third Floor, Lawrenceville, NJ 08648, and indicate the form and question number(s) or circumstances as well as your name and address.

*When will I receive my score report?*

Allow approximately four weeks from the date of testing to receive your score report. Allow six to eight weeks to receive a score report for the *Principles of Public Speaking* examination.

*Will my test scores be released without my permission?*

Your test score will not be released to anyone other than the school you designate on your answer sheet unless you write to us and ask us to send a transcript elsewhere. Instructions about how to do this can be found on your score report. Your scores may be used for research purposes, but individual scores are never made public nor are individuals identified if research findings are made public.

*If I do not achieve a passing score on the test, how long must I wait until I can take the test again?*

If you do not receive a score on the test that will enable you to obtain credit for the course, you may take the test again after six months (180 days). Please do not attempt to take the test before six months (180 days) have passed because you will receive a score report marked *invalid* and your test fee will not be refunded.

*Can my test scores be canceled?*

The test administrator is required to report any irregularities to Thomson Prometric. <u>The consequence of bringing unauthorized materials into the testing room, or giving or receiving help, will be the forfeiture of your test fee and the invalidation of test scores.</u> The DSST Program reserves the right to cancel scores and not issue score reports in such situations.

*What can I do if I feel that my test scores were not accurately reported?*

Thomson Prometric recognizes the extreme importance of test results to candidates and has a multi-step quality-control procedure to help ensure that reported scores are accurate. If you have reason to believe that your score(s) were not accurately reported, you may request to have your answer sheet reviewed and hand scored.

The fees for this service are:
- $20 fee if requested within six months of the test date
- $30 fee if requested more than six months from the test date
- $30 fee if a re-evaluation of the *Principles of Public Speaking* speech is requested

The fee for this service can be paid by credit card or by certified check or U.S. money order payable to Thomson Prometric. Submit your request for score verification along with the appropriate fee or credit card information (credit card number and expiration date) to Thomson Prometric, DSST Program, 2000 Lenox Drive, Third Floor, Lawrenceville, NJ 08648. Include your full name, the test title, the date you took the test, and your Social Security number. Candidates will be notified if a scoring discrepancy is discovered within four weeks of receipt of the request.

*What does ACE recommendation mean?*

The ACE recommendation is the minimum passing score recommended by the American Council on Education for any given test. It is equivalent to the average score of students in the DSST norming sample who received a grade of C for the course. Some schools require a score higher than the ACE recommendation.

*Who is NLC?*

National Learning Corporation (NLC) has been successfully preparing candidates for 40 years for over 5,000 exams. NLC publishes Passbook® study guides to help candidates prepare for all DANTES and CLEP exams and almost every other type of exam from high school through adult career.

Go to our website — www.passbooks.com — or call (800) 632-8888 for information about ordering our Passbooks.

---

To get detailed information on the DSST program and DSST preparation materials, visit www.getcollegecredit.com.

If you are interested in taking the DSST exams, call 877-471-9860 or e-mail pnj-dsst@thomson.com.

# Introduction to World Religions

## TEST INFORMATION

This test was developed to enable schools to award credit to students for knowledge equivalent to that which is learned by students taking the course. The school may choose to award college credit to the student based on the achievement of a passing score. The ultimate passing score for each examination is determined by the school. The school is provided with a recommended passing score established by a national committee of college faculty who teach this course. The DSST program is approved by the American Council on Education (ACE), and the ACE provides both a recommended passing score and a recommended number of credits that could be awarded to successful students. Some schools set their own standards for awarding credit and may require a higher score than the ACE recommendation. Students should obtain this information from the institution from which they expect to receive credit.

## CONTENT OUTLINE

The following is an outline of the content areas covered in the examination. The approximate percentage of the examination devoted to each content area is also noted.

### Introduction to World Religions Exam Content Outline

I. **Definition and Origins of Religion – 6%**
   A. Basic dimensions of religion
   B. Approaches to religion

II. **Indigenous Religions – 6%**
   A. Native North American traditions
   B. Native South American traditions
   C. Native West African traditions
   D. Native Middle Eastern traditions
   E. Hellenic and Roman traditions
   F. Shintoism

III. **Hinduism – 10%**
   A. Historical development
   B. Doctrine and practice

IV. **Buddhism – 10%**
   A. Historical development
   B. Major traditions
   C. Doctrine and practice

V. **Confucianism – 6%**
   A. Historical development
   B. Doctrine and practice

VI. **Taoism – 4%**
   A. Historical development
   B. Doctrine and practice

VII. **Judaism – 16%**
   A. Historical development
   B. Denominations
   C. Doctrine and practice

VIII. **Christianity – 18%**
   A. Historical development
   B. Major traditions
   C. Doctrine and practice

IX. **Islam – 16%**
   A. Historical development
   B. Major traditions
   C. Doctrine and practice

X. **Religious Movements – 8%**
   A. Before 1000 A.D.
   B. After 1000 A.D.

## REFERENCES

The following references were used to create exam questions and may be useful as study materials. You are not allowed to use these references in the testing center.

1. *A History of the World's Religions*, 12th Edition, 2008, David S. Noss, Prentice Hall/Pearson Education, One Lake Street, Upper Saddle River, NJ 07458, vig.prenhall.com.

2. *Religions of the World*, Tenth Edition, 2007, Lewis Hopfe and Mark Woodward, Prentice Hall/Pearson Education, One Lake Street, Upper Saddle River, NJ 07458, vig.prenhall.com.

## SAMPLE QUESTIONS

All test questions are in a multiple-choice format, with one correct answer and three incorrect options. You may want to review these samples for the type of questions that may appear on the exam.

1. Vedic religion originated with
   A. People who were indigenous to India
   B. Aryans who came to India ca. 1500 B.C.E. from Central Asia
   C. Persians who came to India ca. 700 B.C.E.
   D. Greeks who came to India ca. 300 B.C.E. with Alexander the Great

2. In Hinduism, the term "karma" implies
   A. duty
   B. predestination
   C. action and reaction
   D. good action

3. Theravada Buddhism upholds liberation through
   A. devotion to Brahman
   B. one's own moral efforts and spiritual discipline
   C. divine intercession
   D. worship of Buddha

4. In the Four Noble Truths, the Buddha proclaims that the cause of suffering is
   A. lack of proper teachers
   B. aggression and violence
   C. craving
   D. original sin

5. Which of the following Chinese figures transmitted Confucian teachings?
   I. Mencius (Meng-zi)
   II. Hsun tzu (Xun-zi)
   III. Mo tzu (Mo-zi)
   IV. Chu His (Ju Xi)

   A. I and II only
   B. III and IV only
   C. I, II and III only
   D. I, II and IV only

6. In the Tao Te Ching, Lao Tzu indicates that the best way of living is a life of
   A. passivity
   B. assertiveness
   C. natural simplicity
   D. social commitment

7. The Covenant of Judaism refers to
   A. ancient agreements between Israel and neighboring peoples
   B. a pact initiated by Yahweh with a particular people
   C. a contract among Jewish religious leaders
   D. an agreement negotiated be the Hebrew people and the Egyptians

8. A religious observance commemorating the Exodus is
   A. Mishnah
   B. Passover
   C. Yom Kippur
   D. Rosh Hashonah

9. The New Testament Gospels are primarily
   A. complete biographies of Jesus of Nazareth
   B. summaries of Christian ethics
   C. proclamations of Jesus as Risen Lord and Messiah
   D. eyewitness accounts of four apostles

10. Which of the following is NOT one of the Pillars of Islam?
    A. Muslims are expected to go on a pilgrimage to Mecca at least once in their lives, if financially and physically capable.
    B. Muslims have to seek the intercession of Muhammad to achieve paradise.
    C. Muslims are expected to fulfill their charitable duties.
    D. Muslims have to engage in prayer every day.

**Answers to sample questions:** 1-B; 2-C; 3-B; 4-C; 5-D; 6-C; 7-B; 8-B; 9-C; 10-B.

# HOW TO TAKE A TEST

You have studied long, hard and conscientiously.

With your official admission card in hand, and your heart pounding, you have been admitted to the examination room.

You note that there are several hundred other applicants in the examination room waiting to take the same test.

They all appear to be equally well prepared.

You know that nothing but your best effort will suffice. The "moment of truth" is at hand: you now have to demonstrate objectively, in writing, your knowledge of content and your understanding of subject matter.

You are fighting the most important battle of your life—to pass and/or score high on an examination which will determine your career and provide the economic basis for your livelihood.

What extra, special things should you know and should you do in taking the examination?

I. YOU MUST PASS AN EXAMINATION

A. WHAT EVERY CANDIDATE SHOULD KNOW
Examination applicants often ask us for help in preparing for the written test. What can I study in advance? What kinds of questions will be asked? How will the test be given? How will the papers be graded?

B. HOW ARE EXAMS DEVELOPED?
Examinations are carefully written by trained technicians who are specialists in the field known as "psychological measurement," in consultation with recognized authorities in the field of work that the test will cover. These experts recommend the subject matter areas or skills to be tested; only those knowledges or skills important to your success on the job are included. The most reliable books and source materials available are used as references. Together, the experts and technicians judge the difficulty level of the questions.
Test technicians know how to phrase questions so that the problem is clearly stated. Their ethics do not permit "trick" or "catch" questions. Questions may have been tried out on sample groups, or subjected to statistical analysis, to determine their usefulness.
Written tests are often used in combination with performance tests, ratings of training and experience, and oral interviews. All of these measures combine to form the best-known means of finding the right person for the right job.

## II. HOW TO PASS THE WRITTEN TEST

### A. BASIC STEPS

1) Study the announcement

How, then, can you know what subjects to study? Our best answer is: "Learn as much as possible about the class of positions for which you've applied." The exam will test the knowledge, skills and abilities needed to do the work.

Your most valuable source of information about the position you want is the official exam announcement. This announcement lists the training and experience qualifications. Check these standards and apply only if you come reasonably close to meeting them. Many jurisdictions preview the written test in the exam announcement by including a section called "Knowledge and Abilities Required," "Scope of the Examination," or some similar heading. Here you will find out specifically what fields will be tested.

2) Choose appropriate study materials

If the position for which you are applying is technical or advanced, you will read more advanced, specialized material. If you are already familiar with the basic principles of your field, elementary textbooks would waste your time. Concentrate on advanced textbooks and technical periodicals. Think through the concepts and review difficult problems in your field.

These are all general sources. You can get more ideas on your own initiative, following these leads. For example, training manuals and publications of the government agency which employs workers in your field can be useful, particularly for technical and professional positions. A letter or visit to the government department involved may result in more specific study suggestions, and certainly will provide you with a more definite idea of the exact nature of the position you are seeking.

3) Study this book!

## III. KINDS OF TESTS

Tests are used for purposes other than measuring knowledge and ability to perform specified duties. For some positions, it is equally important to test ability to make adjustments to new situations or to profit from training. In others, basic mental abilities not dependent on information are essential. Questions which test these things may not appear as pertinent to the duties of the position as those which test for knowledge and information. Yet they are often highly important parts of a fair examination. For very general questions, it is almost impossible to help you direct your study efforts. What we can do is to point out some of the more common of these general abilities needed in public service positions and describe some typical questions.

1) General information

Broad, general information has been found useful for predicting job success in some kinds of work. This is tested in a variety of ways, from vocabulary lists to questions about current events. Basic background in some field of work, such as sociology or economics, may be sampled in a group of questions. Often these are principles which have become familiar to most persons through exposure rather than through formal training. It is difficult to advise you how to study for these questions; being alert to the world around you is our best suggestion.

2) Verbal ability

An example of an ability needed in many positions is verbal or language ability. Verbal ability is, in brief, the ability to use and understand words. Vocabulary and grammar tests are typical measures of this ability. Reading comprehension or paragraph interpretation questions are common in many kinds of civil service tests. You are given a paragraph of written material and asked to find its central meaning.

## IV. KINDS OF QUESTIONS

1. Multiple-choice Questions

Most popular of the short-answer questions is the "multiple choice" or "best answer" question. It can be used, for example, to test for factual knowledge, ability to solve problems or judgment in meeting situations found at work.

A multiple-choice question is normally one of three types:
- It can begin with an incomplete statement followed by several possible endings. You are to find the one ending which best completes the statement, although some of the others may not be entirely wrong.
- It can also be a complete statement in the form of a question which is answered by choosing one of the statements listed.
- It can be in the form of a problem – again you select the best answer.

Here is an example of a multiple-choice question with a discussion which should give you some clues as to the method for choosing the right answer:

When an employee has a complaint about his assignment, the action which will best help him overcome his difficulty is to
  A. discuss his difficulty with his coworkers
  B. take the problem to the head of the organization
  C. take the problem to the person who gave him the assignment
  D. say nothing to anyone about his complaint

In answering this question, you should study each of the choices to find which is best. Consider choice "A" – Certainly an employee may discuss his complaint with fellow employees, but no change or improvement can result, and the complaint remains unresolved. Choice "B" is a poor choice since the head of the organization probably does not know what assignment you have been given, and taking your problem to him is known as "going over the head" of the supervisor. The supervisor, or person who made the assignment, is the person who can clarify it or correct any injustice. Choice "C" is, therefore, correct. To say nothing, as in choice "D," is unwise. Supervisors have and interest in knowing the problems employees are facing, and the employee is seeking a solution to his problem.

2. True/False

3. Matching Questions

Matching an answer from a column of choices within another column.

## V. RECORDING YOUR ANSWERS

Computer terminals are used more and more today for many different kinds of exams.

For an examination with very few applicants, you may be told to record your answers in the test booklet itself. Separate answer sheets are much more common. If this separate answer sheet is to be scored by machine – and this is often the case – it is highly important that you mark your answers correctly in order to get credit.

## VI. BEFORE THE TEST

### YOUR PHYSICAL CONDITION IS IMPORTANT

If you are not well, you can't do your best work on tests. If you are half asleep, you can't do your best either. Here are some tips:

1) Get about the same amount of sleep you usually get. Don't stay up all night before the test, either partying or worrying—DON'T DO IT!
2) If you wear glasses, be sure to wear them when you go to take the test. This goes for hearing aids, too.
3) If you have any physical problems that may keep you from doing your best, be sure to tell the person giving the test. If you are sick or in poor health, you relay cannot do your best on any test. You can always come back and take the test some other time.

Common sense will help you find procedures to follow to get ready for an examination. Too many of us, however, overlook these sensible measures. Indeed, nervousness and fatigue have been found to be the most serious reasons why applicants fail to do their best on civil service tests. Here is a list of reminders:

- Begin your preparation early – Don't wait until the last minute to go scurrying around for books and materials or to find out what the position is all about.
- Prepare continuously – An hour a night for a week is better than an all-night cram session. This has been definitely established. What is more, a night a week for a month will return better dividends than crowding your study into a shorter period of time.
- Locate the place of the exam – You have been sent a notice telling you when and where to report for the examination. If the location is in a different town or otherwise unfamiliar to you, it would be well to inquire the best route and learn something about the building.
- Relax the night before the test – Allow your mind to rest. Do not study at all that night. Plan some mild recreation or diversion; then go to bed early and get a good night's sleep.
- Get up early enough to make a leisurely trip to the place for the test – This way unforeseen events, traffic snarls, unfamiliar buildings, etc. will not upset you.
- Dress comfortably – A written test is not a fashion show. You will be known by number and not by name, so wear something comfortable.
- Leave excess paraphernalia at home – Shopping bags and odd bundles will get in your way. You need bring only the items mentioned in the official notice you received; usually everything you need is provided. Do not bring reference books to the exam. They will only confuse those last minutes and be taken away from you when in the test room.

- Arrive somewhat ahead of time – If because of transportation schedules you must get there very early, bring a newspaper or magazine to take your mind off yourself while waiting.
- Locate the examination room – When you have found the proper room, you will be directed to the seat or part of the room where you will sit. Sometimes you are given a sheet of instructions to read while you are waiting. Do not fill out any forms until you are told to do so; just read them and be prepared.
- Relax and prepare to listen to the instructions
- If you have any physical problem that may keep you from doing your best, be sure to tell the test administrator. If you are sick or in poor health, you really cannot do your best on the exam. You can come back and take the test some other time.

## VII. AT THE TEST

The day of the test is here and you have the test booklet in your hand. The temptation to get going is very strong. Caution! There is more to success than knowing the right answers. You must know how to identify your papers and understand variations in the type of short-answer question used in this particular examination. Follow these suggestions for maximum results from your efforts:

1) Cooperate with the monitor

The test administrator has a duty to create a situation in which you can be as much at ease as possible. He will give instructions, tell you when to begin, check to see that you are marking your answer sheet correctly, and so on. He is not there to guard you, although he will see that your competitors do not take unfair advantage. He wants to help you do your best.

2) Listen to all instructions

Don't jump the gun! Wait until you understand all directions. In most civil service tests you get more time than you need to answer the questions. So don't be in a hurry. Read each word of instructions until you clearly understand the meaning. Study the examples, listen to all announcements and follow directions. Ask questions if you do not understand what to do.

3) Identify your papers

Civil service exams are usually identified by number only. You will be assigned a number; you must not put your name on your test papers. Be sure to copy your number correctly. Since more than one exam may be given, copy your exact examination title.

4) Plan your time

Unless you are told that a test is a "speed" or "rate of work" test, speed itself is usually not important. Time enough to answer all the questions will be provided, but this does not mean that you have all day. An overall time limit has been set. Divide the total time (in minutes) by the number of questions to determine the approximate time you have for each question.

5) Do not linger over difficult questions

If you come across a difficult question, mark it with a paper clip (useful to have along) and come back to it when you have been through the booklet. One caution if you do this – be sure to skip a number on your answer sheet as well. Check often to be sure that you have not lost your place and that you are marking in the row numbered the same as the question you are answering.

6) Read the questions
Be sure you know what the question asks! Many capable people are unsuccessful because they failed to read the questions correctly.

7) Answer all questions
Unless you have been instructed that a penalty will be deducted for incorrect answers, it is better to guess than to omit a question.

8) Speed tests
It is often better NOT to guess on speed tests. It has been found that on timed tests people are tempted to spend the last few seconds before time is called in marking answers at random – without even reading them – in the hope of picking up a few extra points. To discourage this practice, the instructions may warn you that your score will be "corrected" for guessing. That is, a penalty will be applied. The incorrect answers will be deducted from the correct ones, or some other penalty formula will be used.

9) Review your answers
If you finish before time is called, go back to the questions you guessed or omitted to give them further thought. Review other answers if you have time.

10) Return your test materials
If you are ready to leave before others have finished or time is called, take ALL your materials to the monitor and leave quietly. Never take any test material with you. The monitor can discover whose papers are not complete, and taking a test booklet may be grounds for disqualification.

VIII. EXAMINATION TECHNIQUES

1) Read the general instructions carefully. These are usually printed on the first page of the exam booklet. As a rule, these instructions refer to the timing of the examination; the fact that you should not start work until the signal and must stop work at a signal, etc. If there are any special instructions, such as a choice of questions to be answered, make sure that you note this instruction carefully.

2) When you are ready to start work on the examination, that is as soon as the signal has been given, read the instructions to each question booklet, underline any key words or phrases, such as least, best, outline, describe and the like. In this way you will tend to answer as requested rather than discover on reviewing your paper that you listed without describing, that you selected the worst choice rather than the best choice, etc.

3) If the examination is of the objective or multiple-choice type – that is, each question will also give a series of possible answers: A, B, C or D, and you are called upon to select the best answer and write the letter next to that answer on your answer paper – it is advisable to start answering each question in turn. There may be anywhere from 50 to 100 such questions in the three or four hours allotted and you can see how much time would be taken if you read through all the questions before beginning to answer any. Furthermore, if you

come across a question or group of questions which you know would be difficult to answer, it would undoubtedly affect your handling of all the other questions.

4) If the examination is of the essay type and contains but a few questions, it is a moot point as to whether you should read all the questions before starting to answer any one. Of course, if you are given a choice – say five out of seven and the like – then it is essential to read all the questions so you can eliminate the two that are most difficult. If, however, you are asked to answer all the questions, there may be danger in trying to answer the easiest one first because you may find that you will spend too much time on it. The best technique is to answer the first question, then proceed to the second, etc.

5) Time your answers. Before the exam begins, write down the time it started, then add the time allowed for the examination and write down the time it must be completed, then divide the time available somewhat as follows:
    - If 3-1/2 hours are allowed, that would be 210 minutes. If you have 80 objective-type questions, that would be an average of 2-1/2 minutes per question. Allow yourself no more than 2 minutes per question, or a total of 160 minutes, which will permit about 50 minutes to review.
    - If for the time allotment of 210 minutes there are 7 essay questions to answer, that would average about 30 minutes a question. Give yourself only 25 minutes per question so that you have about 35 minutes to review.

6) The most important instruction is to read each question and make sure you know what is wanted. The second most important instruction is to time yourself properly so that you answer every question. The third most important instruction is to answer every question. Guess if you have to but include something for each question. Remember that you will receive no credit for a blank and will probably receive some credit if you write something in answer to an essay question. If you guess a letter – say "B" for a multiple-choice question – you may have guessed right. If you leave a blank as an answer to a multiple-choice question, the examiners may respect your feelings but it will not add a point to your score. Some exams may penalize you for wrong answers, so in such cases only, you may not want to guess unless you have some basis for your answer.

7) Suggestions
    a. Objective-type questions
        1. Examine the question booklet for proper sequence of pages and questions
        2. Read all instructions carefully
        3. Skip any question which seems too difficult; return to it after all other questions have been answered
        4. Apportion your time properly; do not spend too much time on any single question or group of questions
        5. Note and underline key words – all, most, fewest, least, best, worst, same, opposite, etc.
        6. Pay particular attention to negatives
        7. Note unusual option, e.g., unduly long, short, complex, different or similar in content to the body of the question
        8. Observe the use of "hedging" words – probably, may, most likely, etc.

9. Make sure that your answer is put next to the same number as the question
10. Do not second-guess unless you have good reason to believe the second answer is definitely more correct
11. Cross out original answer if you decide another answer is more accurate; do not erase until you are ready to hand your paper in
12. Answer all questions; guess unless instructed otherwise
13. Leave time for review

b. Essay questions
1. Read each question carefully
2. Determine exactly what is wanted. Underline key words or phrases.
3. Decide on outline or paragraph answer
4. Include many different points and elements unless asked to develop any one or two points or elements
5. Show impartiality by giving pros and cons unless directed to select one side only
6. Make and write down any assumptions you find necessary to answer the questions
7. Watch your English, grammar, punctuation and choice of words
8. Time your answers; don't crowd material

8) Answering the essay question

Most essay questions can be answered by framing the specific response around several key words or ideas. Here are a few such key words or ideas:

M's: manpower, materials, methods, money, management
P's: purpose, program, policy, plan, procedure, practice, problems, pitfalls, personnel, public relations

a. Six basic steps in handling problems:
1. Preliminary plan and background development
2. Collect information, data and facts
3. Analyze and interpret information, data and facts
4. Analyze and develop solutions as well as make recommendations
5. Prepare report and sell recommendations
6. Install recommendations and follow up effectiveness

b. Pitfalls to avoid
1. Taking things for granted – A statement of the situation does not necessarily imply that each of the elements is necessarily true; for example, a complaint may be invalid and biased so that all that can be taken for granted is that a complaint has been registered
2. Considering only one side of a situation – Wherever possible, indicate several alternatives and then point out the reasons you selected the best one
3. Failing to indicate follow up – Whenever your answer indicates action on your part, make certain that you will take proper follow-up action to see how successful your recommendations, procedures or actions turn out to be
4. Taking too long in answering any single question – Remember to time your answers properly

# EXAMINATION SECTION

# EXAMINATION SECTION
# TEST 1

DIRECTIONS: Each question or incomplete statement is followed by several suggested answers or completions. Select the one the BEST answers the question or completes the statement. *PRINT THE LETTER OF THE CORRECT ANSWER IN THE SPACE AT THE RIGHT.*

1. Christian Fundamentalism is a

    A. Protestant movement that emphasizes the work of the Holy Spirit
    B. Protestant movement that grew up in response to issues of liberalism and modernity
    C. Catholic movement that focuses on methodical study of the Bible
    D. Catholic counter-revolution that reasserts the infallibility of the Papacy

    1.____

2. Which of the three "orientations" of religion seeks union with a reality that is greater than oneself?

    A. Apocalyptic
    B. Prophetic
    C. Mystical
    D. Communal

    2.____

3. Traditional indigenous religions in Africa tend to view the supernatural as a(n)

    A. omnipotent god supplemented and served by lesser spirits, including ancestors and animal spirits
    B. impersonal and unrelated set of natural forces
    C. omnipotent god whom people worship and ask for help
    D. pantheon of gods who share separate but roughly equal powers

    3.____

4. Taoism today currently has about 20 million followers and is centered in

    A. Tibet
    B. Korea
    C. Taiwan
    D. China's Hunan province

    4.____

5. What is the term for letters written in the New Testament for the purpose of instruction, encouragement, and practical advice?

    A. Gospels
    B. Acts
    C. Parables
    D. Epistles

    5.____

6. Which of the following beliefs is shared by Sikhs and Hindus?

    A. The caste system
    B. Polytheism
    C. Reincarnation
    D. Living gurus whose ancestry dates back to founders

    6.____

1

7. The purpose of the Puritan jeremiad was to
    A. instill the values of hard work, honesty, and good citizenship
    B. set a tone of guilt and the need for repentance
    C. separate the elect from the masses for the future Final Judgement
    D. celebrate the living mystery of God

8. Animistic beliefs include the idea that
    A. no clear boundaries exist between the natural and supernatural
    B. nature is superior to the supernatural
    C. animals once existed as human beings
    D. there is one creator who intervenes in both the natural and supernatural

9. The Vedas are believed to have come to ancient members of the priestly class directly from
    A. Brahman
    B. Indra
    C. Agni
    D. Vishnu

10. The Jewish community during the Roman period who retreated to the wilderness in response to apocalyptic visions were the
    A. Sadducees
    B. Essenes
    C. Pharisees
    D. Zealots

11. The "Christianization" of the Roman Empire resulted in each of the following, EXCEPT
    A. several books added to the New Testament
    B. a new emphasis on the final destiny of the individual, rather than of the universe itself
    C. the appointment of Christians to high-ranking, official public positions
    D. the government's return of confiscated church property

12. In addition to the Qur'an, Muslims often look to the hadiths for rules of daily life. The hadiths are best described as
    A. rulings of Muhammad's successors
    B. recollections people have had of Muhammad's words and deeds
    C. the sayings of Muhammad's wife, Khadijah
    D. natural laws

13. Which of the following was a nineteenth-century movement that promoted the idea of emotion or intuition—as opposed to reason—as the source of human understanding?
    A. Revivalism
    B. Enlightenment
    C. Mysticism
    D. Romanticism

14. In many primal religions, a common symbol signifying the center of the universe is the    14._____

    A. egg
    B. mandala
    C. tree of life
    D. heart

15. Which of the following words is an acronym for the three major divisions of the Hebrew Bible?    15._____

    A. Pentateuch
    B. Kethuvim
    C. Tanakh
    D. Torah

16. Among followers of the Baha'i faith, the nine doors and central dome of a house of worship symbolize the    16._____

    A. multiple pathways to God
    B. diversity and unity of humankind
    C. sacraments
    D. ten great Manifestations of God

17. Which of the following is NOT one of Hinduism's Darshana scriptures?    17._____

    A. Brahma sutra
    B. Yoga sutras
    C. Nyaya sutra
    D. Kama sutra

18. The "savior" figure in the Hindu religion is    18._____

    A. Vishnu
    B. Brahma
    C. Shiva
    D. Krishna

19. Which of the following alternative religions emphasizes and celebrates the feminine aspect of the divine?    19._____

    A. Wicca
    B. Rastafarianism
    C. Baha'i
    D. Druidism

20. Which of the following is a branch of Japanese Zen Buddhism that holds enlightenment as a gradual process?    20._____

    A. Jodo Shinsu
    B. Soto
    C. Nishi Hongwanji
    D. Rinzai

21. Historically, the most significant outside influence on Hinduism came from     21._____

    A. China
    B. Britain
    C. Germany
    D. Mongolia

22. For each of the New Testament gospel writers, the central concern of the text is     22._____

    A. Jesus's fulfillment of Hebrew prophecies
    B. Palestine's suffering under the rule of Rome
    C. the suffering and death of Jesus
    D. the parables and other teachings of Jesus

23. The authorized Talmud that is considered to be the dominant version in Jewish theology and law is the     23._____

    A. Babylonian
    B. Roman
    C. Jerusalem
    D. Assyrian

24. The second century belief of some Christians that the three persons of the Trinity are merely different modes or aspects of God, rather than three distinct persons, is known as     24._____

    A. Gnosticism
    B. Sabellianism
    C. Niceaism
    D. Anomoeanism

25. The cornerstone of Confucian ethics is _____ , a supreme virtue representing human qualities at their best.     25._____

    A. xin
    B. hsiao
    C. jen
    D. li

26. The starting point for the Buddhist analysis of the human condition is     26._____

    A. sunyata
    B. dukkha
    C. bhodicitta
    D. jhana

27. A main difference between Buddhism and many of the other major religions is its belief in     27._____

    A. salvation through one's own efforts
    B. life after death
    C. renunciation of the material world
    D. one supreme God

28. The Vedic religion
    I. emphasized the eternal cycle of life, death and rebirth
    II. called for order in nature and society
    III. worshipped multiple gods and goddesses
    IV. emphasized sacrifice

    A. I only
    B. I and III
    C. II, III and IV
    D. I, II, III and IV

29. The oldest form of Tibetan Buddhism is a school known as

    A. Gelug-pa
    B. Nyingma-pa
    C. Sakya-pa
    D. Kagyu-pa

30. Shiite beliefs concerning the Imam Mahdi are analogous to the Christian belief in the

    A. Second Coming of Christ
    B. blessed Trinity of the Godhead
    C. divinity of Christ
    D. virgin birth

31. The earliest known Buddhist scripture, known as the Pali canon, is commonly known as the

    A. Vinaya Pitakas
    B. Tipitaka
    C. sutras
    D. Trikaya

32. Today approximately _____ percent of Japan's population follow both Buddhism and Shinto.

    A. 15
    B. 35
    C. 65
    D. 85

33. An important similarity between Jainism and Sikhism is the

    A. view of the human being as a composite of spirit and matter
    B. practice of vegetarianism
    C. monotheistic deity worship
    D. promotion of ahimsa

34. A sacred text for both Confucianism and Taoism was the

    A. I Ching
    B. Mandate of Heaven
    C. Analects
    D. Tao-te Ching

35. The cult of Mithras

    I. was Christianity's leading competitor in the Roman culture of the first three centuries C.E.
    II. was an all-male religion
    III. practiced baptism
    IV. honored a Persian god born on December 25

    A. I only
    B. I, III and IV
    C. II only
    D. I, II, III and IV

36. In Hinduism, a sannyasin is a person who has

    A. perfected the Ayurvedic techniques of preventing illness, healing the sick and preserving life
    B. renounced worldly goods to live a life of asceticism and seek *moksha,* or liberation from reincarnation, through meditation and prayer
    C. achieved a tantric balance between the desire for worldly pleasures and spiritual aspirations
    D. achieved a yogic oneness of breath, mind, and senses, and the abandonment of all states of existence.

37. Which of the following has NOT had a significant influence on the modern Baha'i religion?

    A. Zoroastrianism
    B. Coptic Christianity
    C. Babism
    D. Persian Shiite Islam

38. Which of the following is NOT a belief common to all Baha'is?

    A. World government
    B. Polytheism
    C. An afterlife
    D. Reconciliation of religion and science

39. In Catholicism, devotions to the saints and to Mary, mother of Jesus, are examples of

    A. breviaries
    B. paraliturgical devotions
    C. monastic orders
    D. sacraments

40. Bodhidharma, an Indian monk who traveled to China in the sixth century C.E., is considered the founder of the _____ school of Buddhism.

    A. Pure Land
    B. Mahayana
    C. Zen
    D. Tibetan

41. The most sacred part of the Hebrew Bible is embodied in the    41.____

    A. Prophets
    B. Talmud
    C. Midrash
    D. Pentateuch

42. To most Zoroastrians, God is symbolized by    42.____

    A. fire
    B. wind
    C. water
    D. the earth

43. Virtues endorsed by Confucius include each of the following, EXCEPT    43.____

    A. loyalty
    B. pride
    C. thrift
    D. ritualization

44. In the third century B.C.E., a group of Jain monks, now known as _____, left northern    44.____
    India to avoid a prophesied famine.

    A. Digambaras
    B. Jinas
    C. Svetambaras
    D. Tirthankaras

45. Which of the following is NOT typically associated with Shinto?    45.____

    A. Family values
    B. Shame
    C. Animal spirits
    D. Fertility

46. The Second Vatican Council, or Vatican II, an ecumenical council of the Catholic church    46.____
    opened under Pope John XXIII in 1962 and closed under Pope Paul VI in 1965, established several major changes in public worship within Catholicism. Which of the following was NOT one of these?

    A. More use of sacred music in nontraditional formats
    B. The substitution of grape juice for wine
    C. Using the vernacular rather than Latin in the liturgy
    D. The simplification of rites

47. According to the Jains, the highest stage of life, short of liberation, is    47.____

    A. birth as a bird
    B. sexual maturity
    C. human birth
    D. parenthood

48. The main proponent of ritualism in early Confucianism was

   A. K'ang Yu-wei
   B. Hsun-tzu
   C. Tung Chung-shu
   D. Mencius

49. Among Muslims, the five daily prayers include each of the following, EXCEPT

   A. zuhr
   B. maghrib
   C. id
   D. 'asr

50. For almost forty years after the crucifixion of Jesus, the Christian proclamation about Jesus, known as the _____, circulated entirely by word of mouth.

   A. kerygma
   B. Mishnah
   C. oral law
   D. Q

## KEY (CORRECT ANSWERS)

| | | | | |
|---|---|---|---|---|
| 1. B | 11. A | 21. B | 31. B | 41. D |
| 2. C | 12. B | 22. C | 32. D | 42. A |
| 3. C | 13. D | 23. A | 33. A | 43. B |
| 4. C | 14. C | 24. B | 34. A | 44. A |
| 5. D | 15. C | 25. C | 35. D | 45. B |
| 6. C | 16. B | 26. B | 36. B | 46. B |
| 7. B | 17. D | 27. A | 37. B | 47. C |
| 8. A | 18. D | 28. C | 38. B | 48. B |
| 9. A | 19. A | 29. B | 39. B | 49. C |
| 10. B | 20. B | 30. A | 40. C | 50. A |

# TEST 2

DIRECTIONS: Each question or incomplete statement is followed by several suggested answers or completions. Select the one the BEST answers the question or completes the statement. *PRINT THE LETTER OF THE CORRECT ANSWER IN THE SPACE AT THE RIGHT.*

1. The Three Refuges, also known as the Three Jewels, of Buddhism—a means of affirming one's commitment to Buddhism—include each of the following, EXCEPT

    A. Buddha
    B. Sangha
    C. Dhukka
    D. Dharma

    1._____

2. Which of the following ceremonies are NOT typically performed by Shinto priests?

    A. Funerals
    B. Weddings
    C. Blessing homes
    D. Exorcisms

    2._____

3. Jewish beliefs that are thought by scholars to be influenced by Zoroastrianism include
    I. the distinction between clean and unclean animals
    II. monotheism
    III. the Last Judgment
    IV. marrying foreign wives

    A. I only
    B. II and III
    C. I, II and III
    D. I, II, III and IV

    3._____

4. The first king of the Hebrew tribes was

    A. Solomon
    B. Moses
    C. Saul
    D. David

    4._____

5. A movement that began in the 1960s, bringing tongues-speaking and other pentecostal elements to the Roman Catholic and mainline Protestant churches, was the _____ movement.

    A. charismatic
    B. ecumencial
    C. evangelical
    D. revivalist

    5._____

6. Which of the following events served to modernize the Roman Catholic Church?

    A. Council of Chalcedon
    B. Counter-reformation
    C. Vatican II
    D. Council of Trent

    6._____

7. Which of the following forms of Tibetan Buddhism is most concerned with the experiential dimension of meditation?

    A. Sakya-pa
    B. Gelug-pa
    C. Kagyu-pa
    D. Nyingma-pa

8. The term used to describe Confucianism that is suffused with Buddhist and Taoist ideas is _____ Confucianism.

    A. Singapore
    B. Han
    C. Ch'ing
    D. Neo

9. In primal religions, the female divine is MOST likely to be symbolized by

    A. spirals and eggs
    B. water and lances
    C. trees and rocks
    D. stars and clouds

10. Historically, Taoist sects have been influenced by
    I. Buddhist rituals
    II. Meditation
    III. Confucian virtues.
    IV. Traditional Chinese medicine or Tai Chi

    A. I and II
    B. II, III and IV
    C. III only
    D. I, II, III and IV

11. In most primal religions, sacred time is best described as

    A. linear and focused on the present
    B. progressive and future-oriented
    C. time spent in worship
    D. cyclical and constantly renewing itself

12. Sitting meditation is a practices whose significance is most pronounced in the _____ school of Buddhism.

    A. Zen
    B. Pure Land
    C. Theravada
    D. Mahayana

13. According to Confucius, the most important element of a strong government is

    A. the faith of the people in their rulers
    B. an adequate food supply
    C. the good will of benevolent gods
    D. a strong military

14. The "women's gospel" in the New Testament is

    A. Luke
    B. Matthew
    C. John
    D. Mark

15. _____ were Christians who believed that Jesus's sacrifice represented an atonement for all human beings, not just the elect

    A. Calvinists
    B. General Baptists
    C. Seventh-Day Adventists
    D. Primitive Baptists

16. Which of the following is a sectarian group that grew out of the sixteenth-century Protestant Radical Reformation?

    A. Quakers
    B. Presbyterians
    C. Mennonites
    D. Calvinists

17. The earliest sacred texts of Hinduism are the

    A. Upanishads
    B. Puranas
    C. Vedas
    D. Aranyakas

18. Which of the following Christian doctrines was taught especially by John Wesley and the Methodists?

    A. Perfectionism
    B. Millenialism
    C. Transubstantiation
    D. Predestination

19. Along with Judaism, Islam forbids

    A. circumcision
    B. eating pork
    C. eating unleavened bread
    D. wearing jewelry

20. The Sadducees, a political/religious sect of the Christian New Testament period,

    A. established the concept of a final judgement
    B. were vehemently opposed to Roman rule in Palestine
    C. practiced a literal reading of the Torah
    D. observed both the "oral law" and the written law

21. The "Four Affirmations" of Shinto include
    I. Self-sacrifice
    II. Physical cleanliness
    III. Tradition and family
    IV. Matsuri, or worship

    A. I and III
    B. II and IV
    C. II, III and IV
    D. I, II, III and IV

22. Which of the following is NOT considered a major prophet in Hebrew scripture?

    A. Malachi
    B. Jeremiah
    C. Joel
    D. Ezekiel

23. The Hindu trimurti is meant to symbolize

    A. goodness, temptation, and evil
    B. creation, preservation, and destruction
    C. man, woman, and child
    D. birth, death, and rebirth

24. Which of the following is a technical theological term in Christianity for acceptability before God?

    A. Justification
    B. Salvation
    C. Grace
    D. Redemption

25. The early statement of Orthodox Christian belief known as the Nicene Creed emphasizes

    A. the truth of Jesse's miracles
    B. the compassion of Jesus for sinners
    C. Jesus' fulfillment of messianic prophecies in the Hebrew Bible
    D. Jesus' equality with God

26. The major contention of Islam against the Baha'i is the belief in

    A. condoning homosexual partnerships
    B. a single world government
    C. an immortal soul
    D. Baha'u'lah as the final prophet

27. Which of the following is a component of the nature of Brahman, the Supreme Being described in the Upanishads?   27._____

    A. Wrath
    B. Jealousy
    C. The feminine essence of life
    D. Joy

28. In the Islamic tradition, Mawlid al-Nabi is a celebration of   28._____

    A. Muhammad's birthday
    B. the day when Abraham intended to follow the instructions of God by sacrificing his son Ishmael
    C. the New Year
    D. the martyrdom of Husain, grandson of Muhammad

29. A Sikh refers to God as   29._____

    A. Guru
    B. Adi Granth
    C. The One
    D. The True Name

30. Which of the following new religions involves an "auditor" to find and remove areas that have created blockages to personal growth?   30._____

    A. Voodoo
    B. Falun Gong
    C. Theosophy
    D. Scientology

31. The Shinto sect with the largest number of adherents today—but which no longer regards itself as a Shinto sect—is _____ Shinto.   31._____

    A. Taikyo
    B. Kurozumikyo
    C. Tenrikyo
    D. Konkokyo

32. Apocalyptic expectations, predicting major changes in the world, are part of the belief system of   32._____
    I. Taoism
    II. Judaism
    III. Zoroastrianism
    IV. Hinduism

    A. I and II
    B. II and III
    C. II, III and IV
    D. I, II, III and IV

33. Of the following gospels, the one that is not part of the new Testament and consists almost entirely of sayings of the risen Jesus is the Gospel of

    A. Thomas    B. Mary    C. Peter    D. Eve

34. The word *Islam* means

    A. seeking
    B. conquest
    C. God
    D. submission

35. Which of the following experiences, associated with forms of Methodism and the holiness tradition, is said to cleanse the individual of a deep-seated sinfulness?

    A. Anointment
    B. Consecration
    C. Sanctification
    D. Aspersion

36. In the Buddhist calendar, the festival of Magha Puja

    A. commemorates the Buddha's birth, enlightenment and final passing away
    B. begins the annual three-month Rains Retreat, when all monks stay inside their monasteries to study and meditate
    C. commemorates the occasion when 1250 disciples gathered spontaneously to hear the Buddha preach
    D. is the most universally celebrated festival in the Buddhist calendar

37. The Upanishads contain teachings on the
    I. conduct of rites
    II. nature of the soul, or atman
    III. nature of oneself
    IV. wartime assistance granted by the god Indra

    A. I and IV
    B. II only
    C. II and III
    D. I, II, III and IV

38. The Islamic calendar measures time from the starting point of

    A. the first of God's revelations to Muhammad
    B. Muhammad's birth
    C. the acceptance of Muhammad's prophethood by Abu Bakr and Umar
    D. Muhammad's migration to the city of Medina

39. Which of the following forms of Buddhism originated in China and spread north to Japan?

    A. Mahayana    B. Pure Land    C. Theravada    D. Zen

40. In early Vedic religion, the most important ritual or belief was      40.____

    A. almsgiving
    B. the sacred thread
    C. the fire sacrifice
    D. puja

41. In raja yoga, the ultimate goal of meditation is a superconscious state in which the mind    41.____
    is totally under control. This state is known as

    A. Moksha
    B. Kripa
    C. Samadhi
    D. Nirvana

42. Sallenkhana, or _____, is valued in Jainism as the noble end to a long life of virtue and    42.____
    detachment.

    A. self-starvation
    B. the achievement of divinity
    C. enlightenment
    D. pilgrimage

43. To the Jain, enlightenment and liberation from the cycle of life and death can only be    43.____
    achieved through

    A. meditation
    B. fruititarianism
    C. salekhana
    D. asceticism

44. Seventeenth-century Massachusetts Bay Puritanism is an example of    44.____

    A. presbyterianism
    B. theocracy
    C. autocephaly
    D. fundamentalism

45. The ancient Sanskrit text known as the Laws of Manu direct orthodox Brahmins to    45.____

    A. honor members of all caste groups
    B. study the Vedas
    C. devote themselves to temple worship
    D. teach salvation through Krishna-worship

46. After a dramatic revelatory event, Sri Guru Nanak Dev founded Sikhism in the fifteenth    46.____
    century as an attempt to

    A. map a new path for enlightenment
    B. stave off the religious oppression of the Punjabi people
    C. reconcile the Hindu and Muslim religions
    D. achieve ritual purification

47. The Latin translation of the Bible known as the Vulgate was composed by

   A. Eusebius Caesarea
   B. Origen
   C. Athanasius
   D. Jerome

48. The "intuitive sects" of Mahayana Buddhism are associated with the idea that
   I. reason should not be trusted
   II. students may achieve enlightenment with the help of koans
   III. the keys to enlightenment are held by compassionate bhodisattvas
   IV. people find enlightenment through meditation

   A. I only
   B. I and II
   C. III only
   D. I, II and IV

49. In ancient China, the most liberal thinkers were typically the

   A. followers of Xunzi
   B. Taoists
   C. Legalists
   D. Confucians

50. Jains among the laity have six basic duties, including
   I. venerating teachers
   II. renouncing certain foods or activities
   III. showing indifference to the body
   IV. studying the teachings of the Tirthankaras

   A. I and II
   B. I, II and III
   C. III and IV
   D. I, II, III and IV

## KEY (CORRECT ANSWERS)

| | | | | |
|---|---|---|---|---|
| 1. C | 11. D | 21. C | 31. C | 41. C |
| 2. A | 12. A | 22. A | 32. C | 42. A |
| 3. C | 13. A | 23. B | 33. A | 43. D |
| 4. C | 14. A | 24. A | 34. D | 44. B |
| 5. A | 15. B | 25. D | 35. C | 45. B |
| 6. C | 16. C | 26. D | 36. C | 46. C |
| 7. C | 17. C | 27. D | 37. C | 47. D |
| 8. D | 18. A | 28. A | 38. D | 48. D |
| 9. A | 19. B | 29. D | 39. A | 49. B |
| 10. D | 20. C | 30. D | 40. C | 50. B |

# TEST 3

DIRECTIONS: Each question or incomplete statement is followed by several suggested answers or completions. Select the one the BEST answers the question or completes the statement. *PRINT THE LETTER OF THE CORRECT ANSWER IN THE SPACE AT THE RIGHT.*

1. An early Muslim criticism of Christianity was that its practitioners    1.____

    A. associated too closely with Jews
    B. violated the doctrine of monotheism through their belief in the Trinity
    C. were overzealous in their conversion practices
    D. were violently intolerant of other religions

2. When Paul of Tarsus traveled to Damascus from Jerusalem, his original intent was to    2.____

    A. arrest prominent members of the Christ-worshipping Jerusalem Church
    B. receive his first communion
    C. gain converts to Christianity
    D. purchase slaves

3. Which of the three "orientations" of religion focuses on rituals and ceremonies as the path to salvation?    3.____

    A. Prophetic
    B. Apocalyptic
    C. Sacramental
    D. Mystical

4. The Druze    4.____
    I. do not accept converts
    II. are not considered Muslims by other Muslims
    III. believe in the spiritual superiority of women
    IV. have kept their doctrine and rituals secret

    A. I and II
    B. I, II and IV
    C. II and III
    D. I, II, III and IV

5. Which of the following philosophies best summarizes the main message contained in the Bhagavad-Gita?    5.____

    A. People should abandon the material world and take up the pursuit of spiritual awakening.
    B. People should perform the duties appropriate to their station, without regard to success or failure.
    C. War cannot be justified on any grounds.
    D. All things are each a part of one Lord, and both men and gods are manifestations of a single Divine Spirit.

6. The most likely reason for the many offshoots from the Shinto religion is its    6._____

   A. lack of a strong organizational structure
   B. ethnic heterogeneity
   C. focus on natural forces
   D. complex, meticulous doctrines

7. Shi'ite Muslims believe that    7._____

   A. Pilgrims should visit the grave of Ali
   B. Ali, like Muhammad, was a prophet
   C. An inner knowledge of Allah can be achieved through meditation, ritual, and dancing
   D. The world will experience an era of justice under the coming mahdi

8. Each of the following is a Taoist value, EXCEPT    8._____

   A. spontaneity
   B. appreciation the movements of nature
   C. simplicity
   D. formal education

9. Christianity's monastic movement began in    9._____

   A. Egypt
   B. Rome
   C. Spain
   D. Constantinople

10. The kingdom of Israel was divided in 928 B.C.E. into two kingdoms, northern (Israel) and southern (Judah). The factor that was most influential in creating this division was    10._____

    A. the invasion of the Assyrians
    B. Jeroboam's re-introduction of idolatric practices in the south
    C. the imposition of high taxes by Solomon's son, Rehoboam
    D. conflicts over the interpretation of Hebrew scriptures

11. Which of the Hindu yogic paths emphasizes rational thought as the path to liberation?    11._____

    A. Jnana
    B. Bhakti
    C. Karma
    D. Raja

12. An important tenet of Taoism is that a person must nurture the breath that has been given them. This vital life force is referred to as    12._____

    A. shen
    B. ch'i
    C. the Tao
    D. yang

13. Most oral religious traditions

    A. make a clear distinction between the natural and supernatural
    B. do not make much distinction between gods and ancestors
    C. are fairly simple sets of basic beliefs
    D. focus on a single High God

14. Mahayana Buddhism today is practiced around the world, but finds its strongest expression in

    A. China
    B. the United States
    C. India
    D. Japan

15. What is the term for a post-Civil War Protestant movement that taught that the Kingdom of God could only be brought about, on earth, through human effort?

    A. Social Gospel
    B. Primitivism
    C. Society of Friends
    D. Recontructionism

16. Religions that have existed as official state religions include
    I. Judaism
    II. Taoism
    III. Hinduism
    IV. Buddhism

    A. I only
    B. I and II
    C. III and IV
    D. I, II, III and IV

17. According to Jain thought, one-sensed beings include
    I. vegetation
    II. insects
    III. water
    IV. earth

    A. I only
    B. I, III and IV
    C. II only
    D. I, II, III and IV

18. In ancient Hinduism, the second-ranking caste consisted of

    A. warriors and nobles
    B. artisans
    C. merchants
    D. priests

19. Which of the following Confucian scholars taught that "apart from the mind, neither law nor object" exists?

   A. Tung Chung-shu
   B. Wang Yang-ming
   C. Chu Hsi
   D. Mencius

20. The Buddha opposed each of the following, EXCEPT

   A. the privileges and powers of the priestly class
   B. detachment
   C. the performance of rituals for gods
   D. strong loyalty to a guru

21. The Liberal Christians, active in Revolutionary War times especially in and around Boston, were the ancestors of modern

   A. Lutheranism
   B. Ecumenism
   C. Quakerism
   D. Unitarianism

22. The Muslim calendar marks time from the starting point of

   A. Muhammad's flight to Yathrib
   B. Muhammad's moment of revelation
   C. the date of Muhammad's death
   D. the date of Muhammad's birth

23. The Calvinist belief in the inability of humans on their own to say or do anything that could merit them salvation was known as

   A. original sin
   B. fruitlessness
   C. total depravity
   D. fallen nature

24. The Hindu texts that serve primarily to provide mystic teachings of the sacrificial religion are the

   A. Puranas
   B. Upanishads
   C. Aranyakas
   D. Brahmanas

25. Which of the following religions emphasizes intuitive feelings and spiritual emotions expressed through ritual, rather than in articles of belief?

   A. Shinto
   B. Confucianism
   C. Buddhism
   D. Taoism

26. It is a Muslim's duty to recite the creed, "There is no God but God and Muhammad is his Prophet"—a saying known as the 26.____

   A. shahadah   B. hegira   C. salat   D. zuhr

27. Which of the following are practices shared by Muslims and Baha'is? 27.____
   I. Fasting
   II. Pilgrimage
   III. Abstinence from alcohol
   IV. Meeting in nine-sides mosques or temples

   A. I only
   B. II, III and IV
   C. I and III
   D. I, II, III and IV

28. The early Christian church historian Eusebius of Caesarea 28.____

   A. was largely a translator of Greek texts
   B. wrote a summary of the general history of the world from the Creation to 725
   C. was not a Christian himself
   D. divided Christian texts into three different categories: acknowledged, disputed, and rejected

29. Although fasting is strongly recommended as an Islamic practice, it is only required during the holiday of 29.____

   A. Al-Hijra/Muharram
   B. Ramadan
   C. Mawlid al-Nabi
   D. Id al-Adha

30. The commandment of ancient Israel that was cited by Jesus as the "greatest commandment" was the 30.____

   A. Mishnah
   B. Shema
   C. Sabbath
   D. Torah

31. Jehovah's Witnesses believe in the Christian doctrine of 31.____

   A. eternal torment of the sinful
   B. resurrection of the soul
   C. the Trinity
   D. Biblical primacy on all matters

32. In Jainism, the first aim of dharma is to 32.____

   A. purify one's character
   B. reach Nirvana
   C. attend to the needs of one's family
   D. avoid harming other beings

33. The Buddhist text known as the Tipitaka contains rules for the community of monks and nuns, known collectively as the

    A. dharmapeda
    B. khandhas
    C. trikaya
    D. sangha

34. Most Muslims believe that Jesus
    I. was resurrected
    II. cured people of illness
    III. was the Messiah
    IV. restored life to dead people

    A. I, II and III
    B. II only
    C. II, III and IV
    D. I, II, III and IV

35. Jains differ from Theravada Buddhists most notably in their

    A. rejection of monastic discipline
    B. belief in ahimsa
    C. belief in reincarnation
    D. celebration of the austerities of Mahavira

36. All major religions tend to have each of the following in common, EXCEPT the belief in

    A. exercising self-control
    B. the manifestation of God in one specific form
    C. submission to the will of the divine
    D. putting others before oneself

37. The Samaritans were a distinct group of Jews who lived between Judea and Galilee, viewed by most other Jews as a(n)

    A. monastic group with apocalyptic visions
    B. priestly upper class who mingled infrequently with most people
    C. alien group who practiced a false version of Judaism
    D. academy of rabbis who developed the beliefs about the contents of the Bible

38. The purpose of mamori in Shinto practice are to

    A. aid in healing and protection
    B. announce the commencement of a rite
    C. purify the mind and body
    D. communicate reverence to the Kami, or deities

39. What was the name of the Calvinist movement that grew from the conviction that Queen Elizabeth's reforms of the Church of England did not go far enough?

    A. Unitarianism          B. Presbyterianism
    C. Radical Reformation   D. Puritanism

40. In the Buddhist calendar, Kathina

    A. occurs at the beginning of the three-month Rains Retreat
    B. is a remembrance of the three most significant events in the Buddha's life
    C. is the largest almsgiving ceremony of the year
    D. is often used as an occasion to make vows and determinations

41. The Hebrew Bible and ancient Mesopotamian legends have several stories in common. Which of the following is NOT one of these?

    A. The Garden of Eden
    B. The story of Noah and the Great Flood
    C. The Tower of Babel
    D. The story of Job

42. The five dress rituals of strict Sikhs include each of the following, EXCEPT

    A. a steel bracelet
    B. uncut hair
    C. a turban
    D. a ceremonial dagger

43. The original words of Zoroaster (Zarathrushtra) are said to be preserved in a series of five hymns known as the

    A. Mithras
    B. Avestas
    C. Amesha Spentas
    D. Gathas

44. Both Taoism and Confucianism are viewed as responses to _____ in ancient China.

    A. ancestor worship
    B. a series of natural disasters
    C. the social, political and philosophical conditions of life
    D. Mongolian invaders

45. The belief system that was closely associated with the Enlightenment and natural religion was

    A. agnosticism
    B. Presbyterianism
    C. Protestantism
    D. deism

46. What is the term for a scroll containing Jewish scripture?

    A. Haggadah
    B. Midrash
    C. Megillah
    D. Bavli

47. Which of the following is an example of apocalyptic writing in the Hebrew Bible?

    A. Genesis
    B. Daniel
    C. 2 Kings
    D. Micah

48. What is the term for a religion that worships only one God, but concedes that other communities have other deities?

    A. Deist
    B. Ecumenical
    C. Henotheist
    D. Theosophist

49. Generally, the hymns of the Rig Veda serve to

    A. praise the gods and ask them for worldly benefits such as wealth, health, long life, and victory in war
    B. give instructions for how to conduct elaborate sacrificial rituals
    C. provide melodies and chants that are to accompany rituals
    D. spell out the doctrines and beliefs of the emerging Vedic religion

50. As set forth in the book of Genesis, the Noahide Code prohibits
    I. having more than one spouse
    II. idolatry
    III. cruelty to animals
    IV. extramarital sex

    A. I and II
    B. I, III and IV
    C. II, III, and IV
    D. I, II, III and IV

## KEY(CORRECT ANSWERS)

| | | | | |
|---|---|---|---|---|
| 1. B | 11. A | 21. D | 31. D | 41. D |
| 2. A | 12. B | 22. A | 32. A | 42. C |
| 3. C | 13. B | 23. C | 33. D | 43. D |
| 4. D | 14. D | 24. C | 34. C | 44. C |
| 5. D | 15. A | 25. A | 35. D | 45. D |
| 6. A | 16. D | 26. A | 36. B | 46. C |
| 7. D | 17. B | 27. C | 37. C | 47. B |
| 8. D | 18. A | 28. D | 38. A | 48. C |
| 9. A | 19. B | 29. B | 39. D | 49. A |
| 10. C | 20. B | 30. B | 40. C | 50. C |

# TEST 4

DIRECTION: Each question or incomplete statement is followed by several suggested answers or completions. Select the one the BEST answers the question or completes the statement. *PRINT THE LETTER OF THE CORRECT ANSWER IN THE SPACE AT THE RIGHT.*

1. In general, which school of Buddhism tends to reject scriptures for more direct methods of gaining insight?

    A. Zen
    B. Theravada
    C. Shingon
    D. Mahayana

1.____

2. The early Christian historian who is considered to be the first real "theologian" in the church was

    A. Jerome
    B. Origen
    C. Eusebius
    D. Clement of Alexandria

2.____

3. In the Jain tradition, the word "Jina" means

    A. liberator
    B. teacher
    C. sufferer
    D. conqueror

3.____

4. Of the following approaches to religion, which stresses an adherence to reason rather than religious authority and attempts to relate answers to a systematic whole?

    A. Psychology
    B. Mysticism
    C. Philosophy
    D. Mythology

4.____

5. The body of text covering rules of Jewish ritual and tradition, enforceable in Jewish courts, is known as the

    A. Halakah
    B. Nevi'im
    C. Haggada
    D. Gemarah

5.____

6. A comparison of Taoism and Confucianism reveals that Taoism is more
    I. individualistic
    II. mystical
    III. influenced by nature
    IV. concerned with social relations

    A. I only    B. I, II and III    C. II and III    D. IV only

6.____

7. The Divine Liturgy of Eastern Christian Orthodoxy, like the Mass of Roman Catholicism, recalls the

    A. prophecy of John the Baptist concerning the Lamb of God
    B. Last Supper of Jesus and his death on the cross
    C. 40-day trial of Jesus in the desert
    D. birth of Jesus at Bethlehem

8. In Hinduism, the power of a god is often denoted by means of

    A. multiple arms
    B. physical size
    C. lightning bolts
    D. rings of fire

9. A word that refers to Christ's "second coming" in Christianity is

    A. revelation
    B. kerygma
    C. rapture
    D. parousia

10. According to the gospel of Mark, Jesus' "two commandments" that summed up his teachings included the commandment to

    A. believe the gospel
    B. be not afraid
    C. be born again
    D. love thy neighbor as thyself

11. Taoist sects often use practices that date from ancient times, including
    I. alchemy
    II. baptism
    III. faith healing
    IV. sacrifice

    A. I only
    B. I and III
    C. II and IV
    D. III only

12. Hermeticism, a philosophy that developed at the end of the Hellenistic era, was based on each of the following, EXCEPT

    A. Roman Christianity
    B. Gnosticism
    C. Astrology
    D. Platonism

13. Wandering Hindu ascetics, like Theravada Buddhist monks,   13.____

    A. wear orange robes
    B. practice elaborate daily rituals
    C. are strict vegetarians
    D. are not required to be celibate

14. Confucian virtues that were later embraced by Mao Tse-tung included   14.____
    I. selfless service to the public
    II. self-improvement for the public good
    III. filial piety
    IV. observance of rituals and propriety

    A. I only
    B. I and II
    C. II and IV
    D. II, III and IV

15. Which of the following movements, religions, or philosophies was NOT associated with millenial beliefs?   15.____

    A. Orthodox Judaism
    B. The nineteenth-century Native American Ghost Dance
    C. Nazism
    D. Anabaptism

16. Lao Tsu's primary motivation for writing the Tao te Ching was to   16.____

    A. offer an alternative to the Confucian view
    B. end the constant feudal warfare and other conflicts of his time
    C. establish a state religion as a means of centralizing authority
    D. elevate himself as the object of a nationwide personality cult

17. Examples of incarnations in the religious experience include   17.____
    I. Buddha
    II. Jesus
    III. Krishna
    IV. Muhammad

    A. I and II
    B. II only
    C. II and III
    D. I, II, III and IV

18. Rastafarians recognize _____ as the promised land.   18.____

    A. Babylon
    B. Israel
    C. Ethiopia
    D. Jamaica

19. The vision quest of many Native American tribes is an example of a(n)

    A. sequestration
    B. act of penitence
    C. direct supplication to a higher power for specific needs
    D. rite of passage

20. Which of the following Greek mythological figures, like Jesus as reported in the New Testament, was born of divine parentage, died a violent death, and spent his afterlife enthroned in heaven?

    A. Odysseus     B. Achilles     C. Orpheus     D. Dionysus

21. Liberal Protestantism, a form of American Protestantism the grew out of the religious pluralism of the later nineteenth century, associated with ideas such as the
    I. significance of the social gospel
    II. humanity of Jesus
    III. inherent goodness of human nature
    IV. work of the Holy Spirit

    A. I only
    B. I, II and III
    C. III only
    D. I, II, III and IV

22. An offshoot of the Puritan movement, committed to a doctrine of the Inner Light and humanitarian 'benevolence' toward all peoples, is the

    A. Restorationists
    B. Shakers
    C. Unitarian Church
    D. Society of Friends

23. As formulated in the Upanishads, the aim of Hinduism is to

    A. signal devotion to one of the many gods
    B. honor social obligations
    C. meditate to understand the essence of reality
    D. form new religious insights by rejecting the Vedas

24. The tenth and final enlightened Guru in the Sikh tradition was the Guru

    A. Ramananda           B. Granth Sahib
    C. Teg Bahadur         D. Gobind Singh

25. A similarity between Jains and Theravada Buddhists is their

    A. ethical requirements for both monks and laity
    B. belief that all attachments bring bondage
    C. evolution into a thriving merchant class
    D. striving for a holy death

26. According to the Jehovah's Witnesses, Christ became King in the year _____ C.E.   26._____

    A. 0
    B. 33
    C. 1054
    D. 1914

27. The Arabic word referring to the community of those who follow Allah is   27._____

    A. Umma
    B. Sunna
    C. Wali
    D. Hadith

28. The teachings of _____, who felt that heretics should be forced to convert to Christianity for the sake of their own salvation, were largely behind the Spanish Inquisition.   28._____

    A. Tomas de Torquemada
    B. Augustine
    C. King Ferdinand
    D. Thomas Aquinas

29. Which of the following Hindu texts consists primarily of magical spells and incantations?   29._____

    A. Aranyakas
    B. Rig Veda
    C. Brahmanas
    D. Atharva Veda

30. The "golden age" of Islamic civilization is usually identified with the   30._____

    A. Umayyad dynasty
    B. Abassid dynasty
    C. return of Muhammad to Mecca
    D. Ottoman Turks

31. "Qur'an" is an Arab word meaning   31._____

    A. Guidebook
    B. Recitation
    C. Scripture
    D. Revelation

32. The Three Marks of Existence in Buddhism include each of the following, EXCEPT   32._____

    A. karuna (compassion)
    B. dukkha (suffering)
    C. anatta ("not-self")
    D. anicca (impermanence)

33. Which of the following New Testament characters, in his words and behavior, seems to share a number of beliefs with the sect known as the Essenes?

    A. John the Baptist
    B. The apostle Paul
    C. Jesus of Nazareth
    D. Judas Iscariot

34. The central theme of the Bhagavad Gita could be best described as

    A. a single pathway to reaching God
    B. penance and atonement
    C. service to both gods and people
    D. renunciation and detachment

35. Which of the following is NOT prohibited by the Sikh religion?

    A. Eating meat
    B. Idol worship
    C. The use of tobacco
    D. The caste system

36. Shinto Grand Festivals (Taisai) include each of the following, EXCEPT

    A. Jidai Matsuri
    B. Aoi Matsuri
    C. Iwashimizu Matsuri
    D. Gion Matsuri

37. Which of the following religious figures is mentioned in the Qur'an?

    A. Buddha      B. St. Paul      C. Baha'u'llah      D. Jesus

38. The purpose of a traditional Native American vision quest is to

    A. connect with a specific totem
    B. see into the future
    C. contact the spirit world and gain insight or power
    D. know the thoughts of other people

39. Shinto generally emphasizes each of the following, EXCEPT

    A. tranquility      B. holiness      C. cleanliness      D. sensibility

40. The main difference between the Samkhya and the Vedanta schools of Hindu thought centers on the

    A. conduct of rites
    B. question of reincarnations
    C. role of worldly pleasures in daily life
    D. number of realities in the universe

41. What is the term for the Wiccan midwinter solstice celebration?

    A. Beltain
    B. Shabbat
    C. Yule
    D. Samhain

42. The Jain principle of aparigraha promotes

    A. chastity
    B. truthfulness in all forms of communication
    C. detachment from one's possession and from other humans
    D. fruititarianism

43. In Theravada Buddhism, the purpose of vipassana is to

    A. make the practitioner see things as they really are
    B. end the cycle of birth and rebirth
    C. remove the five hindrances to the experience of jhanas
    D. allow the Buddha nature emerge naturally from within

44. In the Taoist view, death is a

    A. return to one's ancestors
    B. predictable natural transformation
    C. fearful, evil event
    D. threshold to one's rebirth

45. In the Hebrew tradition, earlier prophets such as Elijah focused on

    A. temple rituals
    B. the sins of worshipping other gods
    C. God's role in political realities
    D. the consequences of social and moral sins

46. The largest Shinto group, with roots dating back to prehistory is _____ Shinto.

    A. Shuha (sect)
    B. Jinja (shrine)
    C. Minzoku (folk)
    D. Koshitsu (Shinto of the Imperial House)

47. The southern kingdom of Judah was conquered in 586 B.C.E. by the

    A. Babylonians
    B. Persians
    C. Assyrians
    D. Egyptians

48. Early Christian believers referred to Jesus by a name that means "anointed one" and that ancient Jews gave to all their kings. The name was  48._____

    A. Yahweh
    B. Apostle
    C. Messiah
    D. Christ

49. In Zen Buddhism, the ultimate purpose of meditation is satori, or  49._____

    A. the ability to help all sentient beings
    B. a flash of insight in to the true nature of reality
    C. rebirth in the Pure Land
    D. perfection of one's own life

50. The Nichiren sect of Mahayana Buddhism is closely associated with  50._____

    A. the Lotus Sutra
    B. Sukhavati
    C. the arhant ideal
    D. Bodhidharma

# KEY (CORRECT ANSWERS)

| | | | | |
|---|---|---|---|---|
| 1. A | 11. B | 21. B | 31. B | 41. C |
| 2. B | 12. A | 22. D | 32. A | 42. C |
| 3. D | 13. A | 23. C | 33. A | 43. A |
| 4. C | 14. B | 24. D | 34. D | 44. B |
| 5. A | 15. A | 25. B | 35. A | 45. B |
| 6. B | 16. B | 26. D | 36. C | 46. B |
| 7. B | 17. C | 27. A | 37. D | 47. A |
| 8. A | 18. C | 28. B | 38. C | 48. C |
| 9. D | 19. D | 29. D | 39. B | 49. B |
| 10. D | 20. D | 30. B | 40. D | 50. A |

# TEST 5

DIRECTIONS: Each question or incomplete statement is followed by several suggested answers or completions. Select the one the BEST answers the question or completes the statement. *PRINT THE LETTER OF THE CORRECT ANSWER IN THE SPACE AT THE RIGHT.*

1. Which of the following is a concept associated with Roman Catholicism?   1.____

    A. Higher law
    B. Monism
    C. Univeralism
    D. Natural law

2. According to Lao Tzu (Laozi), the most important factor determining a person's actions should be   2.____

    A. family and social relationships
    B. personal ambition
    C. the will of the divine
    D. the movement of nature

3. In primal religions, broken taboos are most likely to be repaired through   3.____

    A. rites of confession or penitence
    B. sacrifices
    C. musical and/or dancing ceremonies
    D. the creation of icons

4. Which of the following is NOT a doctrine typically associated with Theosophy?   4.____

    A. Chaos
    B. Duality
    C. Reincarnation
    D. Karma

5. Which of the following ancient Chinese texts was the only one to have been compiled by Confucius himself?   5.____

    A. *Ch'un Ch'iu, or Spring and Autumn Annals*
    B. *I Ching, or Book of Changes*
    C. *Lun Yu, or Analects of Confucius*
    D. *Shu Ching, or Book of History*

6. Jain monks and nuns who fully practice the ascetic life typically   6.____
    I. eat only at night
    II. avoid bathing
    III. extinguish any fires they find
    IV. avoid digging

    A. I only
    B. II and III
    C. III and IV
    D. I, II, III and IV

33

7. Taoist households continue to practice domestic rituals such as the party for the god of the _____ , who presents a yearly report on the family to the Jade Emperor.

   A. the kitchen  B. wealth
   C. the present  D. fire

8. The lasting influence of the Egyptian Cult of Isis on the Roman Church can be seen in the variety of Christianity known as

   A. Arianism  B. gnosticism  C. Marianism  D. ecumenism

9. Which of the following is NOT a belief or practice typical of New Age Americans?

   A. Western norms  B. Numerology
   C. Reiki  D. Yoga

10. Which of the following religions is unique in that during its existence of over several thousand years, it has never compromised on the concept of nonviolence, either in principle or practice?

    A. Shinto  B. Jainism  C. Hinduism  D. Buddhism

11. In the synoptic gospels, material found in Matthew and Luke but not in Mark is known as the

    A. apocrypha
    B. Q
    C. double tradition
    D. Jerusalem perspective

12. Which of the following was NOT a grade of filial piety to one's parents, according to Confucius?

    A. Glorifying them
    B. Not bringing shame to them
    C. Providing for them
    D. Providing grandchildren

13. The Puritans believed
    I. Salvation was from God alone
    II. Christians should only do what was explicitly directed by the Bible
    III. Church and state should remain separate
    IV. God worked through covenants with individuals, communities and churches

    A. I only  B. I, II and IV
    C. II and III  D. I, II, III and IV

14. Probably the most commonly used scriptural texts in the Hindu tradition are the

    A. uranas
    B. Brahmanas
    C. Vedas
    D. Upanishads

15. According to Confucius, the primary importance of rituals is their    15.____

    A. unification of people with the natural world
    B. encouragement of unity among people
    C. sacrificial role in people's relationship to the gods
    D. usefulness in predicting the future

16. An important scripture in the Mahayana Buddhist tradition is the    16.____

    A. Sukhavativyuha scriptures
    B. Lotus Sutra
    C. tantras
    D. Tipitaka

17. Which of the following is currently the world's largest Animistic belief system?    17.____

    A. Hinduism
    B. Neopaganism
    C. Shinto
    D. Buddhism

18. The purpose of the Zen koan can best be described as    18.____

    A. ending the cycle of birth/rebirth
    B. providing rational answers to life's puzzling spiritual questions
    C. invoking a being or phrase that has spiritual significance
    D. jolting the mind out of its habitual thought processes

19. Between what years were the books of the New Testament written?    19.____

    A. 1200-440 B.C.E.
    B. 586-518 B.C.E.
    C. 50-150 C.E.
    D. 367-1517 C.E.

20. Which of the following was a movement within the Christian church that advocated salvation through extraordinary spiritual understandings of heavenly truths that are denied to most people?    20.____

    A. Ebionism    B. Arianism    C. Sabellianism    D. Gnosticism

21. The ancestral deity of the imperial house, who is associated with the sun in Shinto belief, is known as    21.____

    A. Ameratsu Omikami
    B. Susano
    C. Hachiman
    D. Tamayorihime-no-mikoto

22. To Confucius, the most important human relationship was that between a

    A. ruler and subject
    B. friend and a friend
    C. husband and wife
    D. father and son

23. Most Zoroastrians practicing today live in

    A. Iran
    B. the Arabian peninsula
    C. India
    D. Ethiopia

24. In which Buddhist sect or school do members NOT have to rely on their own efforts for liberation?

    A. Zen          B. Theravada          C. Pure Land          D. Tibetan

25. The Hebrew Prophet Isaiah taught that
    I. there is only one God for all the people of the world
    II. scriptures have more authority than prophets
    III. Jews would endure 40 years of suffering for their refusal to take Canaan
    IV. a Messiah was soon to come to the Jews

    A. I only
    B. II and IV
    C. III only
    D. I, II and III

26. Which of the three "orientations" of religion stresses contact with the sacred by proper belief and adherence to moral rules?

    A. Prophetic          B. Communal          C. Sacramental          D. Mystical

27. Islamic beliefs include
    I. Jesus' escape from crucifixion and entrance into Paradise
    II. the existence of Satan, who drives people to sin
    III. the birth of all children into a pure, natural state of submission to Islam
    IV. an official rejection of racism

    A. I and II
    B. II, II and IV
    C. II only
    D. I, II, III and IV

28. The earliest statement of a belief in repeated lives through reincarnation appears in the Hindu text known as the

    A. Rig Veda
    B. Brahmanas
    C. Upanishads
    D. Aranyakas

29. The Book of Malachi appears at the end of most Christian arrangements of Old Testament scriptures because

    A. Malachi was a contemporary of Jesus
    B. it was the last book written in the Hebrew Scriptures
    C. Christians believe Malachi predicted the appearance of John the Baptist
    D. its apocalyptic nature is closest in tone and content to Revelation, the last book of the New Testament

30. Which of the following was a Hebrew family that established an independent Jewish nation that lasted until 63 B.C.E.?

    A. Sadducees
    B. Pharisees
    C. Maccabees
    D. Essees

31. The Radhasoami movement began in 1861 as an offshoot of the _____ religion in India.

    A. Jain
    B. Hindu
    C. Buddhist
    D. Sikh

32. The most likely means of demonstrating respect for a Hindu guru is to

    A. bow in the person's presence
    B. offer the person food
    C. kneel before the person
    D. touch the person's feet

33. According to the Jain religion, matter adheres to the soul because of

    A. fear of death              B. past actions
    C. material desires           D. the acquisition of worldly goods

34. In Buddhism, the "Five Hindrances" to the experience of jhanas–rapturous states resulting from meditation–include each of the following, EXCEPT

    A. anxiety
    B. sloth
    C. lust
    D. not-self

35. The Antimission Baptists believe that missionary work was made unnecessary by the

    A. imminent Final Judgement
    B. innate goodness of human nature
    C. diligent practice of good works and living by spiritual example
    D. Calvinist doctrine of predestination

36. Yoga–the Hindu pursuit of liberation from suffering–has refined itself over the centuries to consist of four primary "paths." The one most familiar to Westerners is raja yoga, which is the path of

    A. love and devotion
    B. self control and self mastery
    C. wisdom and knowledge
    D. selfless service

37. To a Buddhist, Right Understanding determines the intentions we have, so Right Intention determines our actions and behavior. This is one of the teachings of

    A. dukkha
    B. dharma
    C. samsara
    D. karma

38. Paul's most original contribution to the Christian religion was the

    A. conception of Jesus as a messiah who would save humankind from political bondage
    B. belief that Jesus had resurrected and would
    C. conception of the death of Jesus as saving humankind from sin
    D. complete separation of Jesus from Hebrew scriptures

39. Which of the following is a term meaning "the concept of the presence of God in the world?"

    A. Duality
    B. Deism
    C. Incarnation
    D. Immanence

40. Regular practices of most Jains include

    A. animal sacrifice          B. meditation
    C. pilgrimage                D. almsgiving

41. During the Roman period of control over Israel, the Zealots were

    A. separatists who formed an ascetic monastic community
    B. priestly and aristocratic Jews who interpreted Jewish law literally
    C. ritualistic Jews whose teachings spoke of a coming Messiah
    D. a nationalistic Jewish faction with extreme anti-Roman views

42. Huldreich Zwingli, a Swiss radical reformationist of the sixteenth century, rejected several practices of the Catholic church. Which of the following was NOT rejected by Zwingli?

    A. Priestly or monastic celibacy
    B. The worship of saints
    C. The veneration of icons or statues
    D. The confession of sinners to a priest, rather than direct entreaties to God for forgiveness

42.____

43. Sikh founder Guru Nanak presented three central teachings as the path to God. These include each of the following, EXCEPT

    A. sharing one's earnings
    B. offering time in service of others as a sacrifice to God
    C. remembering God as the one true actor and giver
    D. working to earn one's living

43.____

44. Which of the following religious founders said: "There is no Hindu, no Muslim"?

    A. The Buddha
    B. Vhardamana Mahavira
    C. Baha'u'llah
    D. Sri Guru Nanak Dev

44.____

45. In Catholicism and Christian traditions, the prescribed cycle of worship throughout the year–including the structure of the services, the texts for study, and the hymns to be sung–is generally known as the

    A. creed     B. Mass     C. liturgy     D. homily

45.____

46. Which branch of Islam believes that the successor to Muhammad should have been a male directly descended from the prophet's immediate family?

    A. Druze     B. Shi'ite     C. Sufi     D. Sunni

46.____

47. Christian Evangelicalism emphasizes
    I. the personal experience of the grace of God in "rebirth"
    II. the use of the Bible as the primary source of God's revelations
    III. mission work to help promote conversion
    IV. Christ's redemptive work on the cross, especially as the means for salvation and the forgiveness of sins

    A. I only
    B. I and II
    C. II, III and IV
    D. I, II, III and IV

47.____

48. Which of the following texts is NOT considered a basis for the Hindu school of thought known as Advaita Vedanta?

    A. Brahma-sutras
    B. Rig Veda
    C. Upanishads
    D. Bhagavad-Gita

48.____

49. Which of the following "alternative" religions blend aspects of Christianity into their beliefs and practices?

      I. Wicca
      II. Falun Gong
      III. Santeria
      IV. Cao Dai

- A. I only
- B. II and III
- C. III and IV
- D. I, II, III and IV

50. Most African religions hold the belief that earthly death is followed by

- A. rebirth in human or animal form
- B. absorption into the elements
- C. a spiritual afterlife
- D. a judgement by the higher spirits

## KEY (CORRECT ANSWERS)

| | | | | |
|---|---|---|---|---|
| 1. D | 11. C | 21. A | 31. D | 41. D |
| 2. D | 12. D | 22. D | 32. D | 42. D |
| 3. B | 13. B | 23. C | 33. B | 43. B |
| 4. A | 14. A | 24. C | 34. D | 44. D |
| 5. A | 15. B | 25. A | 35. D | 45. C |
| 6. B | 16. B | 26. A | 36. B | 46. B |
| 7. A | 17. C | 27. D | 37. D | 47. D |
| 8. C | 18. D | 28. B | 38. C | 48. B |
| 9. A | 19. C | 29. C | 39. D | 49. C |
| 10. B | 20. D | 30. C | 40. C | 50. A |

# EXAMINATION SECTION
# TEST 1

DIRECTIONS: Each question or incomplete statement is followed by several suggested answers or completions. Select the one that BEST answers the question or completes the statement. *PRINT THE LETTER OF THE CORRECT ANSWER IN THE SPACE AT THE RIGHT.*

1. Which of the following is NOT considered to be one of the world's three great *missionary* religions?

    A. Buddhism
    B. Hinduism
    C. Christianity
    D. Islam

    1.____

2. Islamic doctrine denotes *jinn* as

    A. mortal spirits that are neither human nor angelic in nature
    B. prophets sent by God to spread His teachings
    C. evil spirits sent to tempt the followers of God
    D. mortal infidels

    2.____

3. In the Buddha's lifetime, the political climate in India could BEST be described as

    A. a growing suspicion of religious mysticism
    B. an increasingly rigid caste system
    C. the replacement of tribal republics with territorially based kingdoms
    D. a developing revolutionary attitude of populist self-determination

    3.____

4. Religious Taoism differs most from other religions in that it

    A. makes extensive use of iconography
    B. is not concerned with life after death
    C. it involves magical rituals
    D. advocates a life of inaction

    4.____

5. According to the Hindu tradition, each of the following is one of the three classical aims in life EXCEPT

    A. *moksha,* liberation from the cycle of birth and death
    B. *kama,* sensual pleasure
    C. *bhakti,* living devotion to a deity
    D. *artha,* wealth and power

    5.____

6. The belief that there is one high god that ranks above all others is known as

    A. polytheism
    B. henotheism
    C. monotheism
    D. pantheism

    6.____

7. The term *Torah* has evolved to mean in the Jewish tradition

    A. the first five books of the Hebrew Bible
    B. any written book of law
    C. the entire Hebrew Bible and the books of oral law, including the *Talmud*
    D. a set of laws that govern priestly behavior

    7.____

41

8. In the Buddhist tradition, a *bhodisattva* may best be described as one who

   A. has achieved enlightenment, or nirvana
   B. practices a strict code of asceticism in the hope of garnering spiritual merit
   C. can achieve nirvana but chooses not to do so until all other human beings can be saved
   D. has mastered the Dharma

9. Tribal religions of the native North American Pueblo tribes tell of dark underworld below the earth. In contrast to the earth, this underworld is usually depicted as

   A. the final destination of earthly living beings
   B. an eminently sacred realm of unrealized possibility
   C. an exile for those mortals who do not observe the proper rituals
   D. a kingdom ruled by wicked spirits

10. The 18th-century development of Hasidism by Israel ben Eliezer *(the Baal Shem Tov)* could best be described as a _____ movement within Judaism.

    A. populist           B. conservative
    C. mystical           D. elitist

11. Nearly all forms of Buddhism involve the aim of

    A. the attainment of a perfect love
    B. cultivating a spiritually rewarding life
    C. performing good deeds to ensure a blissful afterlife
    D. creating conditions favorable to personal meditation or spiritual development

12. The liturgical year for Christians begins with

    A. Christmas
    B. Lent
    C. The Feast of the Immaculate Conception
    D. Advent

13. A philosophical argument for the existence of God which is based on evidence of a divine plan is described as

    A. epistolary         B. ontological
    C. teleological       D. episcopal

14. The first of the five pillars of Islam *(iman)* is

    A. ritual prayer              B. almsgiving
    C. the profession of faith    D. the Ramadan fast

15. Most historians believe the most likely reason for the Byzantine emperor Constantine's patronage of Christianity is

    A. his anger at the widespread persecution of Christians
    B. his recognition of the political stability offered by the church's existing hierarchy
    C. the pressures of his family and relations
    D. a revelatory vision of the cross in the heavens

16. The collapse of Jerusalem in 70 CE marked the beginning of the                                             16.____

    A. Diaspora
    B. rabbinic Jewish tradition
    C. Reform movement in Judaism
    D. spread of Christianity into Europe

17. Each of the following was a medieval *mendicant* order which developed in the thirteenth         17.____
    century as a monastic response to the growing wealth and worldliness of the Christian
    church EXCEPT the

    A. Benedictines            B. Carmelites
    C. Dominicans              D. Franciscans

18. The emphasis on *bhakti* or devotion in the Hindu tradition emerged in medieval times in          18.____
    the

    A. Aryan culture of the Indus Valley
    B. non-Aryan culture of the Indus Valley
    C. Dravidian culture of southern India
    D. blending of Hindu and Muslim cultures in northwestern India

19. Of the following religions, which can most defensibly be claimed as having its origins            19.____
    rooted in sociological concerns?

    A. Taoism                  B. Judaism
    C. Islam                   D. Confucianism

20. The earliest body of Jewish Biblical interpretation, developed in the period after 70, is         20.____
    known as the

    A. *Talmud*                B. *midrash*
    C. *Septuagint*            D. *Mishnah*

21. In traditional pre-Confucian Chinese society, most people received their sense of comfort         21.____
    and well-being, along with their fear of shame and dishonor, from

    A. the extensive dogma of ancient and medieval religions
    B. their sense of knowing the Tao
    C. their strong sense of living in a large, powerful family group
    D. their apprehension of a personal god

22. Which of the following is NOT one of the four noble truths proclaimed by the Buddha?              22.____

    A. All existence is suffering
    B. All suffering is caused by sins committed against others
    C. All suffering can be overcome
    D. The way to overcome suffering is by following the eightfold path

23. The medieval Christian theologian who is thought to have been the most influential on             23.____
    the development of the faith was

    A. St. Augustine           B. Erasmus
    C. St. Francis             D. St. Anselm

24. The main difference between the Atharvaveda and the other three Hindu *Vedas* is that it

    A. is probably not of Aryan origin
    B. ends with the *Upanishads*
    C. was composed between 1500 BCE and 600 BCE
    D. is meant to be sung

25. In the Jewish lunar calendar, each year begins with a new moon at around the time of the fall equinox, and is celebrated with the festival of

    A. Rosh Hashanah               B. Purim
    C. Passover                    D. Sukkoth

26. As the Islamic tradition grew, the Arabic term *sunnah* came to denote

    A. any orthodox follower of Islam
    B. the example established by Muhammad
    C. the practices of tribal ancestry
    D. the essential truth of the Qur'an

27. Confucius saw the answer to contemporary problems in the ritualization of life, which was found in the practice of

    A. *li*        B. *ch'i*        C. *chun*        D. *jen*

28. The three main *establishments* to emerge from the Protestant Reformation in sixteenth-century Europe include each of the following EXCEPT

    A. Anglicans                   B. Deists
    C. Calvinists                  D. Lutherans

29. According to the existential philosopher Friedrich Nietsche, religion is a(n)

    A. means by which common people attempt to escape the ordinariness of their lives
    B. harmful remnant of the irrational elements of human beings
    C. attempt to explain the continuities between magic and science
    D. expression of faith that is beyond all rationality and transcends all philosophical expectations

30. The practice of *hijab,* or veiling of women, which is still practiced in some segments of Islamic society, was most likely initiated under the influence of

    A. the dictates of the early caliphs
    B. the natural environment
    C. the Qur'an
    D. eastern Christian or ancient Greek usage

31. Among the native Inuit peoples of the Arctic, the traditional custom of keeping the skins of birds and animals that had been killed for food reflects the belief that

    A. their residual spirituality would help the shaman achieve an ecstatic trance
    B. the creatures' souls might eventually return to inhabit them
    C. it was wicked to waste material that had once contained life
    D. doing so would deter the spirit of the animal from seeking vengeance

32. The use of the halo in Christian iconography is traced back to the artistic traditions of the

    A. Copts
    B. Presbyterians
    C. Hebrews
    D. Byzantines

33. The Neo-Confucianist who most clearly stressed the experience of enlightenment was the philosopher

    A. Chu Hsi
    B. Chou Tun-yi
    C. Wang Yang Ming
    D. Ch'eng Yi

34. The *paritta* ceremonies sponsored by some members of the laity of Theravada Buddhism were intended to

    A. beckon to the spirit of Maitreya
    B. produce the magical power that would assure the well-being of the ceremony's sponsor
    C. strengthen the resolve of participants to avoid self-indulgence
    D. recruit the patronage of new members

35. Each of the following is a standard sacrament associated with the Catholic church EXCEPT

    A. assumption
    B. marriage
    C. ordination
    D. anointing the sick

36. Physical anthropologists generally characterize religion as a

    A. complex series of adaptive social mechanisms that developed as people struggled for survival
    B. means of providing the social order required for people to live and work together
    C. pre-rational mode of consciousness
    D. result of the gradually increasing importance of certain objects to human survival

37. Which of the following best states the distinction between a *prophet* and a *messenger* in the Islamic tradition?
    A prophet

    A. is considered to be a divine incarnation of God
    B. conveys a message that is limited to a specific people and for a particular time
    C. is sent by God with a universally binding sacred law
    D. has physically heard the word of God

38. Which of the following best describes the concept of *dharma* that arose during the early development of the Buddhist religion?

    A. A principle of causality
    B. One's social and moral obligations
    C. A set of eternal truths
    D. A means of attaining nirvana

39. To Confucius, the individual effort required in the proper performance of one's duty was denoted by the term

    A. *jen*
    B. *te*
    C. *wen*
    D. *chun*

40. Abraham's contribution to the tradition of Islam was that he

    A. was willing to sacrifice his own son in submission to God
    B. healed the sick and fed the hungry
    C. warned against the falseness of idol worship
    D. introduced the concept of holy

41. Today, the basic forms of most religious studies are

    A. symbolic
    B. pictographic
    C. linguistic or textual
    D. philosophical or theological

42. The first real Muslim community was founded by Muhammad in

    A. Jiddah        B. Medina        C. Mina        D. Mecca

43. Among many African tribal religions, as in the Dogon culture of west Africa, rites and sacrifices are a means of

    A. restoring order
    B. praising particular gods
    C. reinforcing familial bonds
    D. insuring material success

44. The Christian ritual in which an individual is admitted into participation in the community is

    A. penance                B. baptism
    C. confirmation           D. communion

45. Muslim scholars studying *fiqh* generally seek to understand the

    A. Qur'an's stance on the doctrine of *jihad*
    B. rights and obligations of human beings according to God
    C. sources of Islamic law
    D. key elements of the coming revelation

46. According to Karl Marx, religion is a(n)

    A. tool used by the poor to justify resentment and possibly rebellion against the ruling class
    B. set of superstitions that impede the individual from achieving his or her full potential
    C. futile attempt to symbolically elevate the status and aspirations of humankind
    D. illusory value system used to legitimize the oppression of the poor

47. The Qur'an's characteristic use of pronouns, in which *We* address *you*, is indicative of the

    A. great number of people who were involved in transcribing it
    B. dichotomy that separates God and humans
    C. all-pervading nature of the one God
    D. Prophet's role as transmitter of revelation

48. Theology is probably best defined as the    48.____

    A. use of reason and argument in seeking the truth and knowledge of the nature of things and the principles governing existence
    B. branch of speculative inquiry that deals with such concepts as being, knowing, cause, substance, and identity
    C. formal, systematic attempt to give a rational explanation of a religion's teachings
    D. explanation of religions by the purposes they serve rather than by theoretical causes

49. During the early development of Confucianism, the *age of the hundred philosophers,* or the sixth century BCE in China, the philosophical speculations of scholars and teachers tended to be    49.____

    A. radical and anti-establishment
    B. conservative, yet optimistic
    C. focused almost exclusively on belief rather than ritual
    D. pantheistic

50. Many of the observances associated with the Muslim ritual pilgrimage, or *hajj,* performed in the twelfth month of the Islamic calendar, are performed largely to commemorate    50.____

    A. the generalized practice of almsgiving
    B. certain aspects of Abraham's life
    C. the birth of Muhammad
    D. the fall of Mecca

---

# KEY (CORRECT ANSWERS)

| | | | | | | | | | |
|---|---|---|---|---|---|---|---|---|---|
| 1. | B | 11. | D | 21. | C | 31. | B | 41. | C |
| 2. | A | 12. | D | 22. | B | 32. | D | 42. | B |
| 3. | C | 13. | C | 23. | A | 33. | C | 43. | A |
| 4. | B | 14. | C | 24. | A | 34. | B | 44. | B |
| 5. | C | 15. | B | 25. | A | 35. | A | 45. | B |
| 6. | B | 16. | B | 26. | B | 36. | A | 46. | D |
| 7. | C | 17. | A | 27. | A | 37. | B | 47. | D |
| 8. | C | 18. | C | 28. | B | 38. | C | 48. | C |
| 9. | B | 19. | D | 29. | B | 39. | A | 49. | B |
| 10. | A | 20. | B | 30. | D | 40. | C | 50. | B |

# TEST 2

DIRECTIONS: Each question or incomplete statement is followed by several suggested answers or completions. Select the one that BEST answers the question or completes the statement. *PRINT THE LETTER OF THE CORRECT ANSWER IN THE SPACE AT THE RIGHT.*

1. The Council of Chalcedon, which effectively established the Eastern Orthodox tradition of Christianity, held that Jesus was

    A. two separate persons, one divine and one human
    B. a single person with only a divine nature
    C. a single person with both a divine nature and a human nature
    D. a single person who was wholly human but who communicated directly with God

    1.____

2. Which of the following Hindu deities has become the focus of a doctrine of consecutive incarnations?

    A. Vishnu     B. Brahman     C. Shiva     D. Parvati

    2.____

3. The historical interaction between Taoism and Confucianism is best illustrated by the

    A. development of alchemical Confucian sects
    B. more advanced Taoist doctrines of spirituality
    C. beliefs of Mencius on the state of human nature
    D. incorporation of ethical behavior into Taoist practices

    3.____

4. Despite its relative decline in the world, Buddhism has endured in China and Asia largely as a result of

    A. its interdependence with emerging political ideologies
    B. the attractiveness of its conservative traditions
    C. its newly discovered popularity in the West
    D. its openness to acculturation

    4.____

5. The Neo-Confucian movement was begun in China largely as a response to

    A. a renaissance of superstitious pagan rituals
    B. the increasing influence of Buddhism and Taoist religion
    C. a collectivist political movement
    D. the rebellious doctrines of Mohism

    5.____

6. Which of the four Christian gospels most strenuously advances the declaration of Christ as messiah and savior?

    A. Mark     B. Luke     C. Matthew     D. John

    6.____

7. The actual teachings of Confucius are probably best observed in the

    A. *Shih Ching*     B. *I Ching*
    C. *Analects*     D. *Tao te Ching*

    7.____

8. The Islamic tradition states that the first prophet to erect a shrine in the valley of Mecca was

    A. Ishmael     B. Isaac     C. Abraham     D. Muhammad

    8.____

9. Which of the following statements about the concepts of *jen* and *li* in Confucian thought are TRUE?
    I. *Li* is concerned primarily with a person's inner orientation.
    II. *Jen* is related primarily to social behavior.
    III. *Li* has a clearer association with the concept of loyalty.
    IV. *Jen* was expected primarily of nobles in their dealings with inferiors.
The CORRECT answer is:

   A. I, II
   B. II, IV
   C. I, III, IV
   D. All of the above

9.____

10. In the five books of Moses, God's selection of unlikely figures like David or Deborah as instruments of divine will is interpreted by Jews as an illustration of God's

   A. random selection process
   B. absolute control over history
   C. indifference to social status
   D. love for the weak and uninitiated

10.____

11. The majority of religions account for their origins in _____ terms.

   A. sociological
   B. psychological
   C. anthropological
   D. theological

11.____

12. The destruction of Solomon's temple eventually influenced many changes in the nature of Judaism. Which of the following was NOT one of these?

   A. A generalized transition to an urban, rather than an agricultural lifestyle
   B. A proliferation of reform movements throughout the dispersed peoples
   C. The replacement of the Hebrew language with vernacular Aramaic
   D. The development of the synagogue as an institution

12.____

13. Among native American cultures of the Plains regions, religions generally involve numerous differentiated spirits which can be described in each of the following ways EXCEPT they are

   A. considered synonymous with qualities that can be transformed to other beings or inanimate forms
   B. specific to each part of the natural world
   C. significations of specific tribal ancestors
   D. associated with an animating life principle

13.____

14. In the Theravada Buddhist view, monks and nuns occupied a noble position among the community, and belonged to a special group who had entered one of the four stages of the supraworldly path.
Which of the following was NOT one of these four classes of nobility?
The

   A. bodhisattvas, who would be reborn no more than five times
   B. once-returners, who would be reborn no more than once
   C. non-returners, who would not be reborn again
   D. arhants, who had achieved nirvana

14.____

15. To outsiders, the aspect of certain religions that has historically been most threatening and offensive has been the

    A. utter lack of empirical evidence for their beliefs
    B. gradual gentrification of the priestly class
    C. means by which their adherents have attempted to propagate their beliefs
    D. iconography associated with worship

16. What is the term for the sectarian Hindu practice whose aim is to awaken the power of the Goddess and uniting it with Purusa, the male supreme being?

    A. Raja yoga
    B. Hatha yoga
    C. Kundalini yoga
    D. Bhakti yoga

17. What is the term for the Catholic doctrine that the bread and wine of the Eucharist are at the moment of consecration in the service miraculously transformed into the body and blood of Christ?

    A. Transsubstantiation
    B. Transmogrification
    C. Transfiguration
    D. Investiture

18. According to the Qur'an and Islamic tradition, God's role in human history

    A. is that of a merciful creator who has sent his messages through the one true prophet, Muhammad
    B. is conducted through mortal prophets and messengers who convey his will
    C. prescribes a preordained destiny for each person on earth
    D. is played directly, through self-disclosure, incarnation, and divine punishments

19. Which of the following religions is probably the WEAKEST example of religious syncretism?

    A. *Voodoo* of the Caribbean
    B. The Umbanda of Brazil
    C. The New Age movement of North America
    D. The cargo cults of Melanesia

20. The texts that later became the basis for modern Hindu laws, composed in the first centuries of the Common Era, are the

    A. *kalpas*
    B. *dharmasastras*
    C. *Upanishads*
    D. *pupanas*

21. A philosophical argument that finds proof of God's existence implied in the idea of God itself is described as

    A. teleological
    B. cosmological
    C. ontological
    D. theological

22. Each of the following is considered one of the five major prophets in the Islamic tradition EXCEPT

    A. Moses
    B. Abraham
    C. Jesus
    D. David

23. The holiday of Shavuoth, celebrated in late spring, is historically interpreted by rabbinic Judaism to be a commemoration of the

    A. giving of the Torah on Mount Sinai
    B. victories over the Canaanites
    C. victims of the Holocaust of World War II
    D. second exile

24. Which of the surviving Hindu schools of philosophy focuses on the performance of rituals?

    A. Mimamsa      B. Yoga      C. Vedanta      D. Vaisesika

25. The principal figure to shape the direction of the early Christian church was

    A. Luke      B. John the Baptist    C. Peter      D. Paul

26. Religious scholars would most likely agree that the emperor Asoka's role in the history of Buddhism could most closely be compared with that of _____ in Christianity.

    A. Constantine           B. Herod
    C. Martin Luther         D. St. Thomas Aquinas

27. Which of the following best describes Confucius's understanding of Heaven?

    A. A supernatural realm inhabited by the departed souls of ancestors
    B. A higher power, order, and law that displaced the patterns of former gods
    C. The basis of all change in the world
    D. A way station in which the souls of the departed would lie in wait for ultimate judgment

28. Which of the following historical events forever changed the Muslim faith by making inevitable the formation of the Shi'i tradition of Islam?
    The

    A. expulsion of Jews from Medina
    B. Abbasid revolution
    C. appointment of Ali as fourth caliph
    D. murder of Muhammad's grandson, Husayn, at Karbala

29. Reform Judaism arose in

    A. medieval Europe as a planned compromise to accomodate growing mystical sects
    B. twentieth-century North America with the belief that Jewish life should parallel that of modern American society
    C. post-World War II Israeli society to accommodate the influx of various cultures
    D. eighteenth-century Europe with the belief that Jewish life should parallel that of modern European society

30. Shaktism, the Hindu worship of the Great Goddess, developed in India out of a long interaction with

    A. the building of temples to Vishnu
    B. the practice of kundalini yoga
    C. the worship of Shiva
    D. early Vedic brahmins

31. Each of the following was a factor that led to the initial decline of Buddhism in India EXCEPT the

    A. popularity of the Brahmanic Hindu tradition
    B. isolation and self-sufficiency of monasteries
    C. invasion of Muslim conquerors
    D. official persecution of Buddhists by the Chinese

32. Proponents of psychological theories concerning the origin of religion hold religion to be the result of a(n)

    A. *ad hoc* series of affective responses to emerging patterns in the external environment
    B. series of cognitive attempts to explain and adjust to one's external environment
    C. set of conditioned responses to periods of extreme distress or despair
    D. world view obscured by childhood events

33. The term *qiblah,* in the Islamic tradition, means

    A. the annual pilgrimage to Mecca
    B. a ruling issued by a traditional religio-legal authority
    C. classical Islamic scholastic theory
    D. the direction of Mecca, faced during prayer

34. The Confucian concept of *te,* or virtue, is best understood as

    A. the essence of the Tao, passed on to rules from Heaven
    B. a behavior driven by the compassion of one common being to another
    C. a sacred power inherent in the very presence of the philosopher-king
    D. an ideal unattainable by all but the emperor

35. The historical event of profoundest significance for Christians is the

    A. birth of Jesus
    B. suffering and death of Jesus on the cross
    C. miracle of the loaves and fishes
    D. sermon on the Mount

36. The idea of *chung* in Confucian thought signifies loyalty primarily to one's

    A. family
    B. political allies
    C. own heart and conscience
    D. lover or mate

37. In Buddhism, *karma* can best be described as the principle of

    A. moral causality
    B. the primary goal of the eightfold path
    C. self-reliance
    D. renunciation of worldly pleasures

38. Which of the following Biblical figures finally led the Hebrews into the land of Canaan?

    A. Jacob    B. Joshua    C. Moses    D. David

39. Most students of religion would agree that the Hindu principle of *bhakti* has its counterpart in the Muslim tradition of

    A. Sunnism
    B. Sufism
    C. *Sevener* or Isma'ili Shi'ism
    D. *Twelver* or Imami Shi'ism

40. The emergence of the Vaisnava tradition in Hinduism centered on which of the following developments?
    I. The special responses of certain Krishna worshippers to pressures and needs that arose in later historical periods
    II. The proliferation of tantric sects
    III. The gathering of sympathetic groups around the original users of the *Bhagavad Gita*
    IV. The religious life of a tribal people, the Satvatas

    The CORRECT answer is:

    A. I *only*          B. II, III
    C. I, III, IV        D. I, II, III

41. Of the following Chinese religious philosophers, which was a follower of the Neo-Confucian school of thought?

    A. Hsun-tzu         B. Kao-tzu
    C. Mencius          D. Chang Tsai

42. Which of the following were reasons why the teachings of Muhammad were initially rejected by members of his community?
    I. His teachings undermined the authority of the merchants and political leaders.
    II. They shamed the tribal ancestors.
    III. They slighted the teachings of Abraham.
    IV. They contested the sacredness of tribal ties.

    The CORRECT answer is:

    A. I, II            B. I, III
    C. I, III, IV       D. I, II, IV

43. The 20th century movement to reunite previously separated or alienated branches of Christianity is known as

    A. catechism        B. Unitarianism
    C. ecumenism        D. congregationalism

44. The purpose of the *Puranas* in Hinduism is to

    A. provoke philosophical discussion about the principles of faith
    B. articulate the three ways to liberation from the cycle of rebirths and deaths
    C. praise deities that have become important in the Hindu pantheon
    D. spell out the *karma yoga*

45. The development of Confucianism is probably best described as a religion that grew primarily out of _____ concerns.

    A. economic
    B. sociological
    C. spiritual
    D. psychological

46. The Buddha was able to establish close ties with lay supporters, and thereby strengthen his religion, primarily because

    A. of his personal charisma
    B. the wealth of his family prevented his having to beg from the common people
    C. he insisted on spending the rainy seasons in settlement with the lay community
    D. he was able to enforce strict standards of conduct among his followers

47. The practice of baptizing infants and young children into the Christian faith became the normal practice for Christians in about

    A. 50, in accordance with Paul's wishes
    B. 250, as a zealous rebellion against Roman persecution
    C. 330, after the patronage of Constantine eliminated the personal risk associated with the rite
    D. 1565, in accordance with the Council of Trent

48. In Abraham's covenant with God, what is promised Abraham and his people in return for the performance of their moral duties?

    A. A decisive victory over their enemies
    B. The lands of Canaan
    C. An end to famine
    D. Unending prosperity

49. The central rite of Christianity, which recalls or re-enacts the self-sacrificing death of Jesus, is

    A. the Passion
    B. Confirmation
    C. Epiphany
    D. the Eucharist

50. Classical Islamic tradition asserts that a person's station in paradise will be determined by the

    A. number of pilgrimages undertaken in his or her life
    B. number of verses of the Qur'an he or she has memorized in his or her life
    C. manner of almsgiving practiced throughout his or her life
    D. number of converts he or she has influenced in his or her life

## KEY (CORRECT ANSWERS)

| | | | | |
|---|---|---|---|---|
| 1. C | 11. D | 21. C | 31. D | 41. D |
| 2. A | 12. B | 22. D | 32. B | 42. D |
| 3. D | 13. C | 23. A | 33. D | 43. C |
| 4. D | 14. A | 24. A | 34. C | 44. C |
| 5. B | 15. C | 25. D | 35. B | 45. B |
| 6. D | 16. C | 26. A | 36. C | 46. C |
| 7. C | 17. A | 27. B | 37. A | 47. C |
| 8. C | 18. B | 28. D | 38. B | 48. B |
| 9. A | 19. D | 29. D | 39. B | 49. D |
| 10. B | 20. B | 30. C | 40. C | 50. B |

# TEST 3

DIRECTIONS: Each question or incomplete statement is followed by several suggested answers or completions. Select the one that BEST answers the question or completes the statement. *PRINT THE LETTER OF THE CORRECT ANSWER IN THE SPACE AT THE RIGHT.*

1. The Christian feast that is associated both with the visit of the magi to the infant Jesus and with Jesus's baptism is the

    A. Pentecost  
    B. Ecstasy  
    C. Assumption  
    D. Epiphany

1._____

2. The most pervasive Buddhist influence on Neo-Confucianism in the 14th century is most clearly found in the

    A. insistence on a metaphysical basis for thought and reality  
    B. proliferation of mystical sects and cults  
    C. complete renunciation of worldly desires  
    D. newly-added practice of meditation

2._____

3. Which of the following was a particular belief of the Maitreya cult that developed out of Theravada Buddhism?

    A. The existence of the Buddha as a divine figure  
    B. A hierarchy of six heavens  
    C. The existence of a future Buddha who would come into the world to make nirvana accessible to everyone  
    D. The existence of the Buddha in four distinct bodies

3._____

4. Which branch of Protestantismis known in the United States as *Episcopalianism,* after its form of government by bishops?

    A. Lutheranism  
    B. Anglicanism  
    C. Unitarianism  
    D. Calvinism

4._____

5. Each of the following elements is generally required of a Hindu marriage ceremony in order for it to be considered legal EXCEPT

    A. the gift of the bride by the father  
    B. the seating of the bride and groom on a platform  
    C. the clasping of hands  
    D. taking seven steps together around a fire

5._____

6. Which of the following was historically a school of Taoist philosophy?

    A. Cheng-i  
    B. K'ou Ch'ien-chih  
    C. Hung Lao  
    D. Ch'uan Chen

6._____

7. Arab society before Islam has been characterized as given to indulgence in sensual pleasures, largely because

    A. the Arabs revered the human body as a temple of God  
    B. they had no code to guide them  
    C. they viewed time to be synonymous with death or fate, which would spare no one  
    D. they ignored the teachings of Moses

7._____

56

8.  The primary purpose of most of the medieval Christian crusades was to        8._____

    A.  proselytize in Muslim lands across the Mediterranean
    B.  recover Jerusalem from Muslim control
    C.  recover Constantinople from Muslim control
    D.  dislodge the Muslims from Spain

9.  Historically, the first mention of the Hindu concept of *karma* appeared in the        9._____

    A.  *dharmasastras*          B.  *Upanishads*
    C.  *itihasas*               D.  *Bhagavad Gita*

10. The social ideal of Taoist religion was revealed in the        10._____

    A.  *Three Sovereigns*            B.  *Tao-Te Ching*
    C.  *Classic of Great Peace*      D.  *I Ching*

11. As the tradition of Theravada Buddhism matured, a gap developed between conservatives and liberals that eventually created an entirely new Buddhist tradition. This conflict centered on the issue of the        11._____

    A.  role of women in the monastic tradition
    B.  interpretation of caste by the arhants
    C.  spiritual superiority of monks to lay persons
    D.  divinity of the Buddha

12. In the time of Jesus, the rabbinic Jewish community was wary of messianic movements primarily because        12._____

    A.  they inspired a zealotry that upset the balance of priestly authority
    B.  they exposed the community to Roman response
    C.  the idea of a messiah was unheard of in the Jewish tradition
    D.  Jesus was believed by most to be a fraud

13. Which school of Hindu philosophy considered the *Vedas* to be infallible texts authored directly by God?        13._____

    A.  Mimamsa     B.  Vedanta     C.  Samkhya     D.  Nyaya

14. Which of the following Taoist religious sects emphasized monasticism and asceticism, and is considered the most significant school in late Taoist history?        14._____

    A.  The Way of the Celestial Masters
    B.  Ch'uan Chen
    C.  The Way of Great Peace
    D.  Huang Lao

15. Sufism, the mystical tradition of Islam, grew largely in response to the        15._____

    A.  increasingly conservative and repressive traditions of Islamic society
    B.  growing materialism of Muslim society and its rulers
    C.  economic difficulty faced by many who sincerely desired to perform the *hajj*
    D.  growing progressiveness of Muslim law

16. In what way has the Holocaust of World War II altered Jewish doctrines?

    A. The catalog of food taboos has expanded to exclude many German customs.
    B. The nationalist Zionist movement has been created.
    C. Jews are no longer permitted to undergo martyrdom, no matter how noble the reasons.
    D. The rituals of the Kabbalah are performed entirely in secret.

17. What is the term used to name the indigenous Christians of Egypt?

    A. Nestorians
    B. Jacobites
    C. Copts
    D. Chalcedonians

18. According to the Yogacara school of Buddhism, the path to realization is associated with

    A. breaking a link in the chain of causation
    B. specific techniques that destroy impure dharmas
    C. recognizing the false duality between *samsara* and *nirvana*
    D. the achievement of transcendent physical pleasure

19. Each of the following is one of the Four Books used as the textual basis for Neo-Confucianism EXCEPT the

    A. *I Ching*, or *Book of Changes*
    B. *Analects*
    C. *Book of Mencius*
    D. *Doctrine of the Mean*

20. During a traditional Bar Mitzvah ceremony, which of the following is typically performed or chanted LAST?
    The

    A. congregation delivers the benediction
    B. celebrant recites special blessings which signal the rationale of the event
    C. Sabbath is acclaimed for the beauty and the serenity it brings
    D. celebrant gives thanks for the scriptures of Law and Prophets

21. In Hinduism, the notion of *trimurti*, or *three forms* is manifested by the

    A. three classical aims of life
    B. sign of the mandala
    C. coalescence of the gods Brahma, Vishnu, and Shiva into one form with three faces
    D. three ways of liberation as preached by Krishna

22. Traditional Jewish practices during the religious holiday of Sukkoth are historically interpreted as

    A. recalling the life of the Israelites in a temporary shelter during their migration from Egypt
    B. a strict observance of the Torah's food taboos
    C. a remnant of an ancient crop festival
    D. a commemoration of Abraham, the patriarch

23. Which of the following was the first form of Buddhism to attract North American converts in significant numbers?

    A. Zen
    B. Lamaism
    C. Theravada
    D. Shingon

24. Regarding the soul's or personality status after death, the ancient Hebrews appeared to believe

    A. that life ended permanently with the stopping of the breath
    B. in two different afterlives for the righteous and for sinners
    C. in a complex, hierarchical arrangement of afterlives
    D. that what mattered was continuing to live on this earth through one's progeny

25. Which of the following effects on the Hindu tradition was created by the spread of the *bhakti* movement across the Indian subcontinent?

    A. The increasingly prominent role of woman saints such as Mira
    B. The diminishing function of Sanskrit texts as scripture
    C. An over-reliance on the aim of *kama*
    D. The increasing prominence of tantric sects

26. Of the four Christian gospels, the one that is not considered *synoptic* is the gospel of

    A. Matthew     B. Mark     C. John     D. Luke

27. Which of the following are historical events that occurred in the ninth month of the Islamic lunar calendar, which established it as the holy month of the observance of the Ramadan fast?

    I. Muhammad's victory at the Battle of Badr
    II. The birth of Muhammad
    III. The death of Muhammad
    IV. Muhammad's reception of the Qur'an's first revelations

    The CORRECT answer is:

    A. I, II     B. II, III     C. I, IV     D. I, II, IV

28. Each of the following is one of the human body's *cinnabar fields,* named in Taoist meditative practice, EXCEPT

    A. head     B. chest     C. abdomen     D. limbs

29. In the Islamic tradition, the term *hanif* denotes

    A. the act of remembering God's name
    B. a text containing traditional reports of Muhammad's words and example
    C. a type of pre-Islamic Arab who believed in the existence of one God
    D. the rejection of Islam

30. Probably the most noteworthy historic legacy of the Second Commonwealth of Jews is the

    A. book of *Isaiah*
    B. beginnings of the rabbinic tradition
    C. editing of the first five books of the Bible by the priestly aristocracy
    D. *book of Deuteronomy*

31. What is the term for the belief that all events, including human action, are determined by causes external to human will?

    A. Animism
    B. Nemesism
    C. Determinism
    D. Structuralism

32. In the Christian tradition, the feast observed on the fiftieth day after Easter, commemorating the day the Holy Spirit enabled the apostles to speak in different languages and spread the word of Jesus, is

    A. Epiphany
    B. Shavuoth
    C. Transformation
    D. Pentecost

33. The rabbinic Jewish tradition expresses its rules regarding food taboos in a manner described as *making a fence around the Torah,* or establishing rules to prevent inadvertent violations of Torah statutes.
    Which of the following items are commonly banned from the Jewish table in accordance with this principle?

    A. Pork in any form
    B. Blood sausage
    C. Poultry and cheese served together
    D. Root vegetables

34. Traditional Chinese religion held that an emperor reigned only because

    A. he had been born into the position
    B. he had received the Mandate of Heaven as a reward for his virtue
    C. he had conquered his opponents
    D. a god had chosen to descend, inhabit the emperor's body, and rule from within it

35. In the classical Hindu tradition of the Upanishads, the Supreme Being, who pervades and transcends the human soul (Atman) and the universe, and is ultimately indescribable is

    A. Brahman     B. Vishnu     C. Brahma     D. Shiva

36. According to Confucius, the first step in establishing the proper order of things (Tao) among human beings was to

    A. renounce the existence of spiritual beings
    B. return to the ways of ancestor worship and filial duty
    C. reform government
    D. discontinue superstitious sacrificial rites

37. The Islamic Qur'an often used the term *People of the Book* to denote

    A. secular bureaucrats
    B. Christians and Jews
    C. the transcribers of Muhammad's teachings into the Qur'an
    D. accomplished scholars of the Qur'an

38. Religious scholars generally agree that each of the following is a characteristic common to all religions EXCEPT

    A. little or no distinction between the natural and supernatural
    B. the encouragement of prayer and communication with the gods
    C. the promotion of a moral or ethical code
    D. some degree of distinction between sacred and profane objects, territory, or time

39. In the Bhagavad Gita, Krishna describes three ways to liberation from the cycle of births and death. Which of the following is NOT one of these?

    A. *Jnana*, knowledge
    B. *Bhakti*, devotion
    C. *Karma*, action
    D. *Darsana*, beholding a deity with faith

40. By the medieval period, Sephardic Judaism had come to be identified with the country of

    A. Spain    B. Germany    C. Assyria    D. Poland

41. According to the Islamic tradition, what is symbolized by the white cloth of the *hajj* pilgrim?

    A. The purity of Islamic doctrine
    B. A person's standing with God
    C. The unspoiled soul of the Prophet
    D. The unity and egalitarianism of Islam

42. Perhaps more than any single event, which of the following marks the transition of Judaism from the national cult of an ancient people to the religious heritage of a widely dispersed people?
    The

    A. Exodus from Egypt
    B. discovery of the book of *Deuteronomy* in the temple at Jerusalem
    C. Babylonian invasion and deportation in 586 BCE
    D. expulsion of Jews from Spain in 1492 CE

43. Which of the following is NOT one of Taoist religion's three life principles?

    A. *Shen*, or spirit              B. *Hsin*, or heart and mind
    C. *Ch'i*, or breath              D. *Ching*, or vital essence

44. The important Buddhist doctrine of *anicca* was established during the 3rd and 4th centuries. *Anicca* can best be described as the

    A. universality of suffering
    B. impermanence of all things
    C. importance of the physical body
    D. significance of personal emotions

45. The proliferation of mystical practices and pietism that occurred in the Jewish community was generated in part as

    A. an adaptive response by Jews in Muslim areas to the growth of Sufism
    B. a means of explaining the terrible displacements and hardships the Jews had experienced in Europe
    C. a means of explaining new messianic sects
    D. rebellion against the encroachment of science

46. The important 19th-century Hindu reform movements were most probably undertaken as a result of

    A. increasingly marginal sectarian tantric practices
    B. the enduring influence of Muslim rule
    C. the involvement of foreign colonial powers in local Indian politics
    D. a desire to demonstrate Hindu solidarity to imperial powers

47. With which Buddhist tradition are tantras most clearly associated?

    A. Theravada            B. Mahayana
    C. Vajrayana            D. Zen

48. Which of the following statements represents the difference between Taoist philosophy and Taoist religion? Taoist

    I. philosophers concentrate on spiritual transcendence, while religious Taoists seek physical immortality
    II. religious rituals predated much of Taoist philosophy
    III. philosophers all follow a strict ascetic tradition, while religious Taoists seek an accumulation of power and wealth
    IV. philosophers condemn political rulers, while religious Taoists advocate loyalty

    The CORRECT answer is:

    A. I, II         B. I, IV         C. II, III         D. I, II, IV

49. Which of the Christian gospels makes the clearest and most comprehensive attempt to link Jesus to the portents of Hebrew scripture?

    A. Matthew       B. Mark          C. Luke            D. John

50. Which of the following Jewish religious holidays is celebrated enthusiastically by modern Israelis as a commemoration of victory over foreign oppressors?

    A. The Ninth of Ab       B. Hanukkah
    C. Passover              D. Purim

## KEY (CORRECT ANSWERS)

| | | | | |
|---|---|---|---|---|
| 1. D | 11. C | 21. C | 31. C | 41. D |
| 2. A | 12. B | 22. A | 32. D | 42. C |
| 3. C | 13. D | 23. A | 33. C | 43. B |
| 4. B | 14. B | 24. D | 34. B | 44. B |
| 5. B | 15. B | 25. B | 35. A | 45. B |
| 6. C | 16. C | 26. C | 36. C | 46. C |
| 7. C | 17. C | 27. C | 37. B | 47. C |
| 8. B | 18. B | 28. D | 38. A | 48. B |
| 9. B | 19. A | 29. C | 39. D | 49. A |
| 10. C | 20. A | 30. C | 40. A | 50. B |

# TEST 4

DIRECTIONS: Each question or incomplete statement is followed by several suggested answers or completions. Select the one that BEST answers the question or completes the statement. *PRINT THE LETTER OF THE CORRECT ANSWER IN THE SPACE AT THE RIGHT.*

1. The origins of what eventually came to be the Hindu caste system are generally thought to lie in verses from the

   A. Bhagavad Gita    B. Rigveda    C. Samaveda    D. Ramayana

   1.___

2. The earliest mystical sect of Christianity was probably the

   A. Kabbalah
   B. Gnostics
   C. Holiness churches
   D. Pentecostals

   2.___

3. The Confucian writings of Mencius generally demonstrate a greater emphasis on _____ than the teachings of Confucius.

   A. the Tao
   B. social propriety
   C. the meaning of the term *Heaven*
   D. *yin* and *yang*

   3.___

4. Which of the following is not a commonly drawn distinction between the Theravada and Mahayana traditions of Buddhism? The Mahayana

   A. tradition emphasizes faith in the Buddha, rather than self-effort
   B. tradition believes that one should focus one's efforts not on achieving nirvana, but on saving other human beings
   C. sutras were not purported to be the literal teachings of the Buddha himself, but commentaries on the older Buddhist traditions
   D. tradition conceived of *sunyata,* or emptiness, which implied that the traditional understanding of the dharmas were lacking in self-nature

   4.___

5. The Hindu religious experience identifies certain foods as having the quality of *rajas,* and therefore giving rise to passion and action. Which of the following is not one of these foods?

   A. Poultry    B. Milk    C. Onions    D. Meat

   5.___

6. Each of the following was a branch of Protestant Christianity that emerged in the seventeenth century EXCEPT the

   A. Congregationalists
   B. Baptists
   C. Unitarians
   D. Quakers

   6.___

7. Which of the following best describes the reason for the tensions which existed between Muslims and Jews in Muhammad's first Islamic community?

   A. Muhammad had commanded the Jews to convert to Islam.
   B. Muhammad had appropriated several Jewish practices of faith.
   C. The Jews had rejected Muhammad's claim to be a prophet and the Qur'an's sacredness.
   D. Muhammad had changed the direction of ritual prayer from toward Jerusalem to toward Mecca.

   7.___

8. The Christian regard for the figure of Mary, evidenced by increasing popular devotion, has developed largely from which of the following?
Her
   I. own immaculate conception and sinlessness
   II. standing as the principle feminine point of access to the Trinity
   III. model of sorrow-enduring love

   The CORRECT answer is:

   A. I only   B. I, II   C. II, III   D. I, II, III

9. Which of the following statements best represents the Confucian understanding of the hereafter?
A person

   A. has two souls, one of which upon death is elevated to a world above, and one of which descends into the grave with the body
   B. has one soul which will either rise or ascend upon death according to the virtue of the departed person's life
   C. has one soul, which departs the body to reunite with the great creator upon death
   D. is by nature lacking in any spiritual essence; if it is attained at all, it can only be granted after earthly existence has come to an end

10. Traditional stories of the lives of the Buddha and Christ have in common which of the following?
   I. Temptation by an evil spirit
   II. A period of self-mortification
   III. Official persecution
   IV. Abandonment by a group of disciples

   The CORRECT answer is:

   A. I, II   B. II, IV   C. I, II, III   D. I, II, IV

11. Which of the following tribes most clearly contributed to the development of the rabbinic Jewish tradition?

   A. Maccabees   B. Sadducees   C. Pharisees   D. Samaritans

12. Of the following noted political slogans involved in the forriative years of the United States, which is most reflective of Taoist philosophy?

   A. *Give me liberty or give me death*
   B. *No taxation without representation*
   C. *That government is best which governs least*
   D. *All men are created equal*

13. The emerging prominence of the Hindu deities Shiva and Vishnu is considered to have begun

   A. with the composition of the Ramayana
   B. during the era of the emperor Gupta
   C. during the era of the emperor Asoka
   D. upon the establishment of an Aryan culture in the Indus Valley

14. In his letters to the Corinthians, Paul asserts that God's primary purpose in sending Jesus was

    A. the liberation of people from their sinful nature
    B. to assure the poor and marginalized that they had a place in God's plan
    C. to give them a new idea of God's love and benevolence
    D. to undermine the Roman bureaucracy

14.___

15. Sigmund Freud, the 20th century psychoanalyst, saw religion primarily as

    A. a misguided attempt to achieve immortality
    B. primitive totemic beliefs dressed up as doctrine and elaborate ritual
    C. a pathological illusion of the immature
    D. the only means of achieving self-actualization

15.___

16. What is the term for the content of instruction administered to candidates for conversion to the Christian faith?

    A. Catechism
    B. Apostolicism
    C. Ecumenism
    D. Epiphany

16.___

17. One of the most significant theories regarding the composition of the Pentateuch, or the five books of Moses, is the Documentary Hypothesis, which states that the books

    A. consist of two major blocks of material written by different authors at different times
    B. consist of four major blocks of material written by different authors at different times
    C. were written by a single priestly group of scholars about two centuries after the death of Moses
    D. were written by numerous priests who lived under Solomon's rule

17.___

18. The *ideal man* in Confucian thought was of a person who

    A. had earned honor through personal effort or individual merit
    B. was entirely free from material desires
    C. had attained enlightenment
    D. had inherited his noble status from birth

18.___

19. Which of the following statements offers the best distinction between the Islamic concepts of *shari'ah,* Islam's sacred law, and *fiqh*?
    *Fiqh* is

    A. *shari'ah* in its contemporary form
    B. the process by which *shari'ah* is interpreted
    C. a more mystical strain of *shari'ah*
    D. the domain of mortals, while *shari'ah* is divine

19.___

20. In contrast with most other religions, the Taoist religion believes that punishment for one's wrongdoings

    A. have a direct effect on how long one lives on earth
    B. is eventually received through rebirth
    C. is nonexistent; misfortunes and accidents are part of nature's spontaneity
    D. is warned from Heaven by disasters or catastrophes

20.___

21. According to the classical Buddhist theory of the later sutras, the Way or eightfold path brought the realization of nirvana by means of

    A. physical suffering
    B. breaking the conventional chain of causation in human existence
    C. improving one's karmic destiny
    D. worshipping the Buddha

22. In the Taoist tradition, the principle of *wu wei* denotes the

    A. path of least resistance, allowing nature to run its course
    B. process of sitting and forgetting one's physical self
    C. power of an individual to effect change
    D. material or vital force at work in the universe

23. According to non-dualist interpreters of the Vedanta school of Hindu philosophy (followers of Sankara), the *m* sound in the sacred syllable om symbolizes the

    A. waking experience  
    B. dream experience
    C. sleep experience  
    D. state of liberation

24. The expositors of Chuang Tzu's school of Taoist philosophy developed the theory that human nature is

    A. naturally perfect; good and evil behaviors are a departure from the original nature
    B. inherently evil, as is evidenced by the desires for good food and sleep
    C. neither good nor evil, but could become either depending on what is learned by an individual
    D. fundamentally good and different from that of other animals

25. The Islamic tradition defines each of the following as one of the sources of Islamic jurisprudence, or *fiqh*, EXCEPT

    A. the *sunnah* of Muhammad and his companions
    B. proclamations by a single contemporary imam
    C. the Qur'an
    D. the consensus of the Muslim community

26. The Roman Catholic Church's efforts to recruit the allegiance of Christians in the Eastern Orthodox world subsequently produced the churches known as _____ churches.

    A. Ecumenical  
    B. Uniate
    C. Apostolic  
    D. Unitarian

27. For the forty years after Moses led the Exodus of Hebrews fron Egypt, they lived primarily

    A. at the foot of Mount Sinai
    B. around Mount Zion, or the Temple Mount
    C. a nomadic life in the wilderness
    D. in the lands of Canaan

28. The religious scholar considered to be the most important to the consolidation of Confucian progress during the Han dynasty was

   A. Kuo Hsiang
   B. Tsang Shan
   C. Tung Chung-shu
   D. Fan Hsu

29. The wandering yogis associated with the Vajrayana ethos developed magical practices that focused on

   A. the complete absence of self
   B. self-mortification
   C. performing one's moral and social duties
   D. the importance of the human body

30. Which of the following texts is NOT considered one of the original Five Classics of Confucianism?
    The

   A. *I Ching,* or *Book of Changes*
   B. *Lun-yu,* or *Analects*
   C. *I-li,* or *Book of Songs*
   D. *Shang Shu,* or *Book of History*

31. The most conclusive reason given to explain the low standing of women in early Arab society has been the

   A. generalized hedonism that preceded Islam
   B. common Islamic practice of female infanticide
   C. words of the Qur'an
   D. status of the society as either a trading or pastoral society, where the role of women was limited

32. The Jewish festival of _____ is traditionally interpreted by a liturgy known as the Haggadah.

   A. Yom Kippur
   B. Rosh Hashanah
   C. Hanukkah
   D. Passover

33. Students and scholars of comparative religion would most likely argue that the role played by Jesus as Christ in the Christian tradition is most like that of the role played by _____ in the Islamic tradition.

   A. Abraham
   B. the Qur'an
   C. Moses
   D. Muhammad

34. The core of Martin Luther's challenge to the Roman Catholic Church in 1517 was

   A. political, focusing on the corruption of church officials
   B. psychological, focusing on the people's motivations for belief in Christ
   C. sociological, focusing on the economic dichotomy promoted by the church
   D. theological, focusing on the nature of sin and redemption

35. In the Hindu tradition, *dharma* means

    A. the principles presented in the *Bhagavad Gita*
    B. a master set of inalienable truths
    C. the continuing cycle of rebirths
    D. one's religious and social duty

36. A philosophical position that gained a considerable following after the eighteenth-century Enlightenment in Europe, which held that God was a creator who had shaped the universe and then abandoned it to run on its own, was known as

    A. Pietism
    B. Deism
    C. Revivalism
    D. Gnosticism

37. The major divisions of Judaism as they are practiced in contemporary society differ primarily in terms of

    A. the habit of observance
    B. belief or doctrine
    C. ethnicity
    D. ritual and practice

38. Confucianism's strongest defense against the status quo was

    A. an initially widespread aristocratic following
    B. the claim that it was trying to return to the original way of doing things
    C. its emphasis on humaneness and compassion
    D. its emphasis on the transmission of virtue from the ruling class

39. Each of the following is an element of the eightfold path preached by the Buddha EXCEPT

    A. aspirations
    B. speech
    C. self-mortification
    D. mindfulness

40. Though Confucius himself did little to address the issue of good and evil, Mencius asserted that

    A. people were without an inclination toward good or evil; their goodness was determined entirely by family teaching and example
    B. people were essentially good; evil behaviors were due to contact with a wicked environment
    C. evil was inherent in human nature
    D. people were beyond such concerns if they practiced

41. The yogic school that emerged during the later development of Mahayana Buddhism followed the doctrine of the *trikaya,* or three bodies of Buddha. Which of the following was NOT one of the bodies included in the *trikaya*?
    The

    A. dharmakaya, considered to be ineffable and indescribable
    B. sambhogakaya, or enjoyment body
    C. nirmanakaya, or magical appearance body
    D. shajakaya, which constituted the unity and essence of the others

42. In the Jewish tradition, the children of a deceased person honor the memory of the dead by reciting a special prayer, the _____ , daily for a year.

    A. Kaddish
    B. Humash
    C. Haggadah
    D. Shema

43. Which of the following is given by the groom to the bride during a Hindu wedding ceremony, and corresponds to a wedding ring in Western society?
    A

    A. necklace or string
    B. double cord, hung from the shoulder
    C. bracelet
    D. veil

44. Which of the following is a reason for the triumph of Confucianism as the imperial ideology of the Han dynasty in China (202 BCE - 220 CE)?
    I. It did away with many pagan rituals.
    II. It provided a firm basis for cultural unity and stability.
    III. It did not require the harsh methods characteristic of the Ch'in dynasty.
    The CORRECT answer is:

    A. I only
    B. III only
    C. I, II
    D. II, III

45. The *surahs* or chapters of the Qur'an are arranged

    A. mechanically, in approximate order of length
    B. thematically
    C. in decreasing order of significance
    D. chronologically

46. Which of the following was the first Chinese philosopher to prompt an upper-class movement away from the Confucian insistence on pagan rituals?

    A. Mencius
    B. Wang Yang Ming
    C. Mo-tzu
    D. Hsun-tzu

47. Historically, the *ten lost tribes* of Israel were dispersed

    A. in the confusion following Solomon's death in 921 BCE
    B. by the Assyrian invasion of 722 BCE
    C. by the Babylonian invasion of 586 BCE
    D. after the Jews' expulsion from Spain in 1492 CE

48. The most distinct difference between the Buddhist bhodisattva and the Neo-Confucian sage was that a

    A. bhodisattva was spoken of as having achieved enlightenment
    B. bhodisattva was content to dwell in contemplation of the eternal principle
    C. sage was active on the world of affairs and was subject to emotion
    D. sage was concerned with the psychological insight into the mental mechanisms by which human beings functioned

49. Of the following Sunni Muslim schools still existing in contemporary society, the _____ school practices the most conservative doctrine.

   A. Hanafite
   B. Malakite
   C. Hanbalite
   D. Safi'ite

49._____

50. The purpose of the *upanayana* ceremony in the Hindu tradition is to

   A. invoke the good favor of Vishnu
   B. initiate a young boy into the stage of a student of Hinduism
   C. proclaim the laws of Manu
   D. mark the passage of a girl into womanhood

50._____

# KEY (CORRECT ANSWERS)

| | | | | |
|---|---|---|---|---|
| 1. B | 11. C | 21. B | 31. D | 41. D |
| 2. B | 12. C | 22. A | 32. D | 42. A |
| 3. C | 13. B | 23. C | 33. B | 43. A |
| 4. C | 14. A | 24. A | 34. D | 44. D |
| 5. B | 15. C | 25. B | 35. D | 45. A |
| 6. C | 16. A | 26. B | 36. B | 46. D |
| 7. C | 17. B | 27. C | 37. D | 47. B |
| 8. C | 18. A | 28. C | 38. B | 48. C |
| 9. A | 19. B | 29. D | 39. C | 49. C |
| 10. D | 20. A | 30. B | 40. B | 50. B |

# TEST 5

DIRECTIONS: Each question or incomplete statement is followed by several suggested answers or completions. Select the one that BEST answers the question or completes the statement. *PRINT THE LETTER OF THE CORRECT ANSWER IN THE SPACE AT THE RIGHT.*

1. Rabbinic Judaism specifies three conditions for the conversion to Judaism. Which of the following is NOT one of these conditions?   1.___

    A. Accepting the burden of the commandments
    B. Circumcision for men
    C. Undergoing a *mitzvah* ceremony
    D. Ritual immersion or baptism

2. During the 3rd and 4th centuries B.C., the sphere of Buddhism's influence began to greatly expand, largely because of   2.___

    A. the support of the Gupta dynasty
    B. its adoption by the emperor Asoka
    C. the reform movement brought about by progressive sects
    D. its growth among people of the Far East

3. The central organizing concept in the Israelite religion was   3.___

    A. Torah    B. the Talmud    C. the Covenant    D. Mishnah

4. A Hindu who marks his or her forehead with three horizontal stripes of white ash is demonstrating devotion to the deity   4.___

    A. Ganesa    B. Shiva    C. Hanuman    D. Vishnu

5. Which of the following is considered the father of Taoist religion?   5.___

    A. Chang Ling    B. Ko Hung    C. Lao Tzu    D. Chuang Tzu

6. In modern times, the Islamic *hadith* tradition has become for many groups, most prominently the Kharijis, a summons for   6.___

    A. the *hajj*
    B. reforming the role of women in Islamic society
    C. stricter Muslim dietary laws
    D. social and religious *jihad*

7. The medieval Christian theologian who presented the *cosmological* argument for God's existence was   7.___

    A. Thomas a Becket        B. Anselm
    C. Hildegard of Bingen    D. Thomas Aquinas

8. Of the following Muslim groups, which tends to express the clearest belief in predestination?   8.___

    A. Shi'i    B. Mu'tazili    C. Sufi    D. Sunni

9. In traditional Chinese religion, each of the following animals is a sign of order in the world EXCEPT the

   A. fox   B. phoenix   C. dragon   D. tortoise

10. In the Sufi Muslim tradition, a Muslim's greatest attainment in his or her relationship to God can best be described by analogy. In the highest sense, a Muslim seeks to become God's

    A. brother or sister
    B. slave
    C. pupil
    D. lover

11. The tradition of Judaism appears to have adopted the doctrine of resurrection in response to

    A. the problem of martyrdom
    B. later Christian influences
    C. later Muslim influences
    D. Moses's encounters with God

12. In the nineteenth and twentieth centuries, the greatest challenge to the spread of Buddhism in Southeast Asia has been the

    A. settlement of Chinese populations in Vietnam and Malaysia
    B. wars in Indochina and Vietnam
    C. infiltration of Christianity from European colonists
    D. overthrow of Cambodian Prince Norodom Sihanouk

13. According to the Five Agents school of ancient Chinese philosophy, the agent of earth had direct power over the element of

    A. metal   B. fire   C. water   D. wood

14. In the Jewish tradition, the ups and downs that have been experienced by Israelites and Jews in history are interpreted as

    A. part of a natural process that corresponds to the agrarian cycle
    B. the result of obedience or defiance of the covenant
    C. clues to the authenticity of their prophets
    D. the whims of a capricious God

15. Neo-Confucianism first became an officially established religion during the _____ dynasty in China.

    A. Ming   B. Han   C. Yuan   D. Sung

16. Today, regions of southern India generally have religious minorities that are better integrated than in the north.
    What is the most likely reason for this?

    A. South India is more homogeneously Dravidian in its ethnicity.
    B. South India has been free of major foreign invasions.
    C. Even the most marginalized sects are fairly moderate in the south.
    D. There has been relatively little Muslim influence in the south.

17. The earliest and most straightforward of the Christian gospels, which begins with the narration of Jesus's mature ministry, is the gospel of

    A. Luke      B. Matthew      C. John      D. Mark

18. According to the Vajrayana tradition of Buddhism, the pantheon of Buddhas, bhodisattvas, and their acolytes

    A. resided within every human being
    B. constituted a very small number
    C. were celestial beings
    D. resided in a distinct geographic location that could be located through the practice of yoga

19. The attribution, common to many primal religions, of a living soul to inanimate objects, plants, or natural phenomena is known as

    A. incarnationism    B. personification    C. animism    D. avatarism

20. In the Hindu tradition, a practice making use of physical and mental discipline to attach one's spirit to a god is comnonly known as

    A. yoga      B. karma      C. tantra      D. bhakti

21. Which branch of Protestantism became known in England as *Presbyterianism,* after its form of government by elders or *presbyters*?

    A. Lutheranism    B. Anglicanism    C. Puritanism    D. Calvinism

22. The important Buddhist doctrine of *anatman* was established during the 3rd and 4th centuries. *Anatman* can best be described as the

    A. nonexistence of any kind of self
    B. universality of suffering
    C. insignificance of the physical body
    D. impermanence of all things

23. The synagogue, rather than the temple, became the focus for *all* Jews as the place of study, assembly, and prayer after the

    A. Babylonian conquest of 596 BCE
    B. conquest of Jerusalem in 70
    C. 1492 expulsion from Spain
    D. Holocaust of World War II

24. A characteristic of primal religions involving a relationship between a person or group and some natural object, phenomenon, or species, is

    A. animism    B. syncretism    C. totemism    D. tropism

25. Probably the most popular god in all of modern Hinduism, the remover of all obstacles and hindrances, is

    A. Hanuman    B. Murukan    C. Ganesa    D. Devi

26. Each of the following is one of the *Five Relationships* spoken of in the Confucian tradition, EXCEPT  26._____

   A. master and slave  
   B. father and son  
   C. ruler and minister  
   D. husband and wife

27. In riany African tribal religions, such as that of the Yoruba of western Africa, the description and expression of divinity corresponds closely to the  27._____

   A. current climate
   B. surrounding topography
   C. surrounding fauna
   D. society's social structure

28. Most of the hymns of the Hindu *Vedas* are petitions for  28._____

   A. a place with the deity in the afterlife
   B. material rewards
   C. an escape from the cycle of rebirths and deaths
   D. a good and happy life on this earth

29. According to the traditional Christian doctrine, the most important element in assuring one's salvation is  29._____

   A. good works  
   B. faith  
   C. predestination  
   D. asceticism

30. The Jewish tradition asserts that God's expectations for the moral conduct of humanity were initially revealed in a covenant with  30._____

   A. Noah   B. Abraham   C. Moses   D. David

31. According to the religion of Australian natives, a person's spirit  31._____

   A. resumes its eternal walk along the songlines of its ancestors upon the person's death
   B. is born with the person and never dies
   C. is elevated to the realm of the master creator, the Rainbow Snake, after death
   D. exists before birth, and remains on or in the land after death

32. During the Western Chou period (1122-771 BCE), three ideas implicit in early Chinese religious attitudes and practices were clearly articulated. Which of the following was NOT one of these?  32._____

   A. The interaction of *yin* and *yang* as the basis of change
   B. Tao as the ultimate ordering principle in the world
   C. The doctrine of *wu wei,* or passivity
   D. Heaven as the impersonal sacred power

33. According to the Islamic perspective, Christians made a fundamental error in  33._____

   A. becoming introverted and exclusive
   B. failing to adopt the teachings of Muhammad
   C. proselytizing
   D. elevating a human being to a level that belongs to God alone

34. Taoist philosophy asserts that the greatest advantage to implementing the principle of *wu wei* is that it

    A. enables the weak to overcome the powerful
    B. allows the mind to completely forget the fact of one's physical existence
    C. creates physical mastery over oneself
    D. allows one to achieve longevity

35. In Hindu temples, the god Shiva is typically portrayed as a(n)

    A. *vimana,* or small tower
    B. monkey
    C. *linga,* or upright phallic shaft
    D. elephant-headed entity

36. Jews consider the holiest of all annual holidays to be

    A. Rosh Hashanah	B. Passover
    C. Yom Kippur	D. Hanukkah

37. During the nineteenth and twentieth centuries, the traditional shari'ah law of Islam

    A. were gradually replaced in the Muslim world by modern legal codes based on Western models
    B. became gradually more progressive, favoring Shi'ite doctrines
    C. made an attempt to accommodate radical sects such as the Druze
    D. remained much the same in accordance with Sunni doctrines

38. Most of the Jews who were expelled from Spain in 1492 migrated to

    A. Germany
    B. Latvia
    C. the Ottoman Turkish Empire
    D. Maghreb

39. In contrast to the unknowable Supreme Being presented by the classical Upanishads, the deity portrayed by lord Krishna in the *Bhagavad Gita* is a(n)

    A. trickster
    B. indifferent creator
    C. loving friend of human beings
    D. wrathful god

40. The Christian sect whose members in the United States refuse to salute the flag or serve in the military, on the grounds that they see themselves as citizens of another kingdom, are the

    A. Christian Scientists	B. Jehovah's Witnesses
    C. Pentecostal Church	D. Seventh-Day Adventists

41. Of the following Hindu texts, which take the form of philosophical conversations between a teacher and student, husband and wife, or fellow philosophers? The

    A. *Bhagavad Gita*	B. *Atharvaveda*
    C. *Upanishads*	D. *puranas*

42. The Confucian view of the state can best be described as

    A. *top-down,* with the common people influenced by the virtuous example of leaders
    B. egalitarian
    C. *bottom-up,* with the leaders following the virtuous example of the masses
    D. *top-down,* with the common people molded through sanction and punishment for wrongdoings

43. On which of the following were the Buddha's teachings most clearly founded?

    A. A willingness to subjugate oneself to the favor of the gods
    B. The recognition of a single supreme being
    C. An intuitive vision achieved through meditation
    D. A divine revelation

44. In contemporary Chinese society, candidates for the Taoist clergy must meet each of the following requirements EXCEPT they must

    A. be males
    B. be under thirty
    C. have family approval
    D. be unmarried

45. The prevalence of abortion in contemporary Hindu society is indicative of

    A. distorted tantric principles
    B. a tendency toward sex selection
    C. the infiltration of Western customs
    D. a loose interpretation of the *dharma* texts

46. For most Christians, the time of year for the greatest solemnity, most serious reflection, and strictest discipline is

    A. Christmas Day
    B. the Epiphany
    C. Lent
    D. Advent

47. The purpose of a shaman in primal religions is primarily to

    A. serve as a physical healer
    B. serve as an intermediary between the world of practical necessity and the spirit world
    C. enforce social laws and taboos
    D. act as a sage deciding political and familial matters

48. Which of the following is associated with the development of Mahayana Buddhism?

    A. A growing conflict between the monastic and lay traditions of Buddhism
    B. Increasingly loose interpretations of the sutras
    C. The emergence of an extensive pantheon of celestial Buddhas, bhodisattvas, and sacred lands
    D. The chanting of mantras

49. The principal text of the mystical Jewish sect, the Kabbalah, is known as the

    A. Dead Sea scrolls
    B. *Mishnah*
    C. *spherot*
    D. *Zohar*

50. Unlike most established world religions, most primal religions center on the question of   50. ____
    A. truth
    B. sensual desires
    C. power over life and death
    D. good vs. evil

---

## KEY (CORRECT ANSWERS)

| | | | | |
|---|---|---|---|---|
| 1. C | 11. A | 21. D | 31. D | 41. C |
| 2. B | 12. C | 22. A | 32. C | 42. A |
| 3. C | 13. A | 23. B | 33. D | 43. C |
| 4. B | 14. B | 24. C | 34. A | 44. A |
| 5. A | 15. D | 25. C | 35. C | 45. B |
| 6. D | 16. B | 26. A | 36. C | 46. C |
| 7. D | 17. D | 27. D | 37. A | 47. B |
| 8. D | 18. A | 28. D | 38. C | 48. C |
| 9. A | 19. C | 29. B | 39. C | 49. D |
| 10. D | 20. A | 30. A | 40. B | 50. C |

# EXAMINATION SECTION
# TEST 1

DIRECTIONS: Each question or incomplete statement is followed by several suggested answers or completions. Select the one that BEST answers the question or completes the statement. *PRINT THE LETTER OF THE CORRECT ANSWER IN THE SPACE AT THE RIGHT.*

1. Which of the following is a Christian sect which stresses the expectation of the Second Coming of Christ?  1.____

    A. Mormons    B. Revivalists    C. Adventists    D. Pentecostals

2. Which of the following is a Muslim festival devoted to the giving of the Qu'ran to Muhammad?  2.____

    A. Lailat-ul-Qadar    B. Id al-fitr
    C. Lailat-ul-Bara'h    D. Ramadan

3. Each of the following concepts can be found in the ancient religion of Zoroastrianism EXCEPT  3.____

    A. the Armageddon battle at the end of this era
    B. the arrival of the Messiah
    C. reincarnation
    D. judgment at death

4. The solemn and central part of the Christian Mass, beginning with the Preface, is the  4.____

    A. liturgy    B. anaphora    C. antiphon    D. homily

5. In the Shinto tradition, *kami* is  5.____

    A. the tradition of revering one's ancestors
    B. a form of meditation used to achieve enlightenment
    C. the spiritual or godlike essence that exists in all things
    D. the doctrine of utmost loyalty to family and principles

6. What is the term for one who converts from one faith to another?  6.____

    A. Evangelical    B. Acolyte    C. Penitent    D. Proselyte

7. What is the term for the highest ranking Anglican bishop in a district or group of dioceses?  7.____

    A. Rector    B. Curate    C. Primate    D. Archbishop

8. The original *dhimmis*, according to the Qu'ran, included  8.____
    I. Jews
    II. Christians
    III. Hindus
    IV. Zoroastrians
    The CORRECT answer is:

    A. I, II    B. I, II, III    C. IV *only*    D. I *only*

9. Which of the following offers the best definition of *adhideha* in the tradition of Indian thought?

   A. Spiritual development and liberation
   B. That which is diametrically opposed to dharma
   C. A virtuous woman
   D. An incarnation finer than the human one, temporarily inhabited by those in the spirit world

10. After Palestine's restoration to Yahweh after the exile, it was sometimes referred to as

    A. Anna     B. Beulah     C. Nazareth     D. Canaan

11. The Zoroastrian tradition suffered its biggest setback when

    A. Alexander the Great conquered Persia
    B. most practitioners emigrated to India
    C. the Muslims conquered Persia
    D. Christianity spread throughout Persia

12. What is the term for a Christian practitioner who is similar to a monk, but is not bound to a single community?

    A. Mendicant     B. Deacon     C. Abbot     D. Friar

13. One who calls the Muslim faithful to prayer from the minaret of a mosque is known as a(n)

    A. imam     B. muezzin     C. purdah     D. mullah

14. Which of the following terms is used to signify Hindu teachings which are orthodox or adhere to the literal rendering of sacred text?

    A. Bhakti     B. Gaya     C. Nyaya     D. Astika

15. Most Sikhs themselves would describe the source of their religion as

    A. a blend of Hindu and Islamic traditions
    B. the divine inspirations of their first Guru and the nine who followed him
    C. a divine text written by God and given as a gift to certain Punjabi tribes
    D. a code that arose from the repulsion of Mughal invaders from the Punjab

16. Which of the following churches is characterized by a doctrine based on a conglomeration of Christian and Taoist ideas?

    A. Unification Church          B. Society of Friends
    C. Shingon                     D. Unitarian Church

17. Among the following, the principle of asceticism is probably LEAST important to

    A. Hinduism                    B. Roman Catholicism
    C. Judaism                     D. Theravada Buddhism

18. What is the term for the Islamic group who believes that successors to the caliphate should be chosen directly and without question by themselves?

    A. Companions    B. Unmayads    C. Legitimists    D. Seveners

19. Which of the following religious traditions is oldest in its origins?

    A. Confucianism    B. Buddhism    C. Taoism    D. Shinto

20. In the early Christian Church, a love feast or communal meal of thanksgiving was known as a(n)

    A. paschal    B. philophus    C. liturgy    D. agape

21. Which of the following is a difference between the Islamic and Jewish rituals of circumcision?
    The

    A. Jewish rite is a rite of initiation
    B. Islamic rite occurs at a later age
    C. Jewish rite cannot be delayed for any reason
    D. Islamic rite is explicitly required in scripture

22. The sacred flame offered in a lamp to the gods during Hindu services is the

    A. arti    B. durga    C. varna    D. agni

23. Which of the following best expresses the roots of Shinto religion?

    A. Confucianism
    B. Ancient tribal mythology
    C. Chinese Buddhism
    D. The Japanese warrior code

24. In Hinduism, there are 64 deities who are attendant on Shiva, and who dwell in an ethereal dimension of being and preside over enlightenment. What are these deities called?

    A. Damayantis    B. Abhasvaras
    C. Bhaktis       D. Sangitas

25. The ultimate goal of Jain practitioners could best be described as liberation through

    A. omniscience      B. redemption
    C. enlightenment    D. faith

26. A *synod* in the Christian tradition is

    A. a member of another religion
    B. a manifestation of God
    C. the highest ranking bishop in a district or diocese
    D. an ecclesiastical council

27. Guru _____ was the founder of Sikhism.

    A. Govind Singh    B. Nanak
    C. Kabir           D. Angad

28. Which of the following is NOT a book of the Old Testament Apocrypha?

    A. Wisdom    B. Malachi    C. Ecclesiasticus    D. Tobit

29. The term *satori* in Buddhism refers to

    A. a shrine in the shape of a mound or dome
    B. the sudden achievement of enlightenment
    C. a Buddha of *immeasurable light*
    D. meditation in the lotus position

30. Which of the following Christian sects is noted for congregation members who *speak in tongues* during a service and who claim to have the gift of healing or prophecy?

    A. Society of Friends           B. Jehovah's Witnesses
    C. Pentecostal Church           D. Seventh-Day Adventists

31. The _____ aspect of a religion is the one which most directly indicates the way in which people's lives are shaped by religion and by which religious institutions operate.

    A. mythological    B. social    C. doctrinal    D. experiential

32. Each of the following was an element of Japan's State Shinto doctrine prior to its 1945 demise EXCEPT the

    A. divine creation of the empire of Japan
    B. state of Japan as an emblem of good surrounded by evil
    C. divine origin of the Japanese people
    D. descent of the emperor from the sun goddess

33. Which of the following religions most clearly has its roots in Aryan culture?

    A. Jainism    B. Hinduism    C. Islam    D. Christianity

34. Which of the following is a divine name used in the Hebrew Bible to substitute for the unutterable name?

    A. Jehovah    B. Adonai    C. Elohim    D. Yahweh

35. Among Christianity's seven cardinal virtues, which is NOT a *theological* virtue?

    A. Hope    B. Faith    C. Justice    D. Love

36. What is the term for the standing prayer recited at all Jewish services?

    A. Kaddish    B. Adonai    C. Shema    D. Amidah

37. The religious tradition of Jainism rose out of

    A. an objection to Hinduism's caste system and its expanding number or deities
    B. a cultural resistance to influence by Mughal invaders from the west
    C. the tribal mythologies of people in the Indus Valley
    D. a feeling that the teachings of Buddhism were becoming distorted beyond their original essence

38. The monastic rule that is generally followed in the Eastern Orthodox Church, encouraging strict observance of religious life but discouraging fanaticism, is the Rule of

   A. Scholastica
   B. Theodore
   C. Benedict
   D. St. Basil

39. According to the *samkhya* school of Hindu thought,

   A. reality is dual in nature, consisting of nature and innumerable eternal souls
   B. the universe goes through alternating periods of creation and destruction
   C. nature is the product of a personal Creator who arranges constituent atoms
   D. by performing appropriate sacrifices, one can assure himself of heavenly rewards

40. The term *Bhagavan,* meaning *Blessed One,* is most often used by Hindus to refer to the god

   A. Hanuman   B. Vishnu   C. Shiva   D. Brahma

41. In a Christian service, what is the term for a prayer of supplication recited by a clergy, alternating with replies from the congregation?

   A. Vespers   B. Litany   C. Plainsong   D. Lauds

42. The first section of the Jewish *Mishnah* is devoted to

   A. ritual purity laws
   B. agricultural laws and benedictions
   C. civil laws
   D. holy things

43. The practitioners of the Baha'i faith are generally expected to do each of the following EXCEPT to

   A. pray or perform service work daily
   B. fast at specified times of the year
   C. undergo an initiation ritual
   D. abstain from alcohol

44. When a religion is criticized by scholars or observers as *ritualistic,* the meaning is that it

   A. draws heavily from primal or pagan traditions and does not focus on more long-term spiritual concerns
   B. lacks a strong doctrine that will give it an enduring form and develop a lasting habit in the lives of adherents
   C. is needlessly harsh in its restrictions on the activities and lifestyles of its adherents
   D. is preoccupied with the motions of observance rather than the intentions and sentiments which give them meaning

45. What is the Jewish code which states which foods are kosher?

   A. Kashrut   B. Haggadah   C. Ezrat   D. Humash

46. Which of the following terras is used to denote present-day practitioners of Zoraoastrianism?

   A. Yasnas   B. Parsis   C. Yazatas   D. Dakhmas

47. What is the term for the early Christian writers (mainly 2nd century) who engaged in reasoned defenses of the Christian faith?

    A. Gnostics  B. Apologists  C. Crucians  D. Disciples

48. How often is *puja*, or worship, performed by Orthodox Hindus?

    A. Once a week
    C. Daily
    B. Three times a week
    D. Three times a day

49. Differences between the two dominant sects of Jainism—the Svetambaras and the Digambaras—include the position of each on
    I. nakedness
    II. the role of women
    III. vegetarianism
    IV. reincarnation
    The CORRECT answer is:

    A. I, II  B. II, III  C. III, IV  D. II, IV

50. In Christianity, the abandonment of one's faith is known as

    A. anathema  B. blasphemy  C. heresy  D. apostasy

## KEY (CORRECT ANSWERS)

| | | | | |
|---|---|---|---|---|
| 1. C | 11. C | 21. B | 31. B | 41. B |
| 2. A | 12. D | 22. A | 32. B | 42. B |
| 3. C | 13. B | 23. B | 33. B | 43. C |
| 4. B | 14. D | 24. B | 34. B | 44. D |
| 5. C | 15. B | 25. A | 35. C | 45. A |
| 6. D | 16. A | 26. D | 36. D | 46. B |
| 7. C | 17. C | 27. B | 37. A | 47. B |
| 8. A | 18. B | 28. B | 38. D | 48. D |
| 9. D | 19. D | 29. B | 39. A | 49. A |
| 10. B | 20. D | 30. C | 40. B | 50. D |

# TEST 2

DIRECTIONS: Each question or incomplete statement is followed by several suggested answers or completions. Select the one that BEST answers the question or completes the statement. *PRINT THE LETTER OF THE CORRECT ANWER IN THE SPACE AT THE RIGHT.*

1. What is the collective term by which the Sikh community calls itself?   1.____

   A. Khalsa   B. Granth   C. Sakhi   D. Panth

2. In Judaism, a commandment or duty, or a good deed or charitable act, is denoted by the term   2.____

   A. sheitel   B. kashrut   C. mitzvah   D. targum

3. The inviolability of monkeys among Hindu people is associated with the cult of   3.____

   A. Hanuman   B. Krishna   C. Ganesha   D. Rama

4. One of the three major elements in the Buddhist way or path is the task of meditation and concentration, or   4.____

   A. sila   B. prajna   C. marga   D. samadhi

5. The Zoroastrian *naojote* ceremony finds its closest parallel in the   5.____

   A. Jewish festival of Sukkoth
   B. Christian confirmation
   C. Sun Dance of the plains tribes of Native Americans
   D. Islamic *hajj*

6. The most severe Muslim sin of putting anything on par with Allah is known as a(n)   6.____

   A. zakat   B. slight   C. agni   D. shirk

7. According to Buddhism, the things and persons that make up the world have three marks. Which of the following is NOT one of these?   7.____

   A. Impermanence          B. Determination
   C. Absence of self       D. Suffering

8. Which of the following is a term meaning *the elevation of a mortal human being to that of a god or goddess*?   8.____

   A. Anthropomorphism      B. Apotheosis
   C. Canonization          D. Transubstantiation

9. The social dimension of Buddhism is represented primarily by the Order of monks and nuns, or   9.____

   A. Triratna   B. Arhants   C. Sangha   D. Dukkha

10. The Pure Land sect of Chinese Buddhism promised salvation to those who call in faith on the name of the great Buddha. What was the Japanese name for this sect?   10.____

    A. Tariki   B. Amida   C. Konkokyo   D. Zen

85

11. What is the term for an Orthodox Christian's prayer to a saint requesting that they pray directly to God on their behalf?

    A. Passion  B. Antiphon  C. Canticle  D. Intercession

12. Which of the following is the Buddhist term for the continuing process of birth and death, for life after life, in many differing forms and conditions of existence?

    A. Samsara  B. Moksha  C. Nibbana  D. Karma

13. Which of the following is NOT generally an element of the spirit of the Benedictine Order?
    A

    A. strictly unified pattern of ritual and observance among all monasteries in the Order
    B. special concern for liturgy
    C. focus on teaching and parochial duties as well as contemplation
    D. special vow attaching them to a specific abbey that is a monk's home for life

14. In which of the following countries or regions is the *Greater Vehicle* of Buddhism predominant?

    A. Sri Lanka  B. Thailand  C. Korea  D. Burma

15. The passover meal commemorating the Israelites' escape from Egypt is the

    A. matzah  B. seder  C. tefillin  D. pesach

16. Which of the following ideas was/were included in the philosopher Mo Tzu's criticisms of Confucianism?
    I. The emphasis on family loyalty could degenerate into a wider selfishness.
    II. The emphasis on love and charity could leave one vulnerable to exploitation.
    III. Confucians were in general too preoccupied with ritual.
    IV. Confucians did not give due weight to a ruler's need to consider the need of other rulers and their subjects.

    The CORRECT answer is:

    A. I, II
    B. I, III, IV
    C. III *only*
    D. II, IV

17. Which of the following historical figures was appointed to be the speaker for Moses on certain occasions?

    A. Malachi  B. Aaron  C. Eleazar  D. Levi

18. Description of the Sikh True God, or Sat Nam, would include each of the following EXCEPT

    A. benign  B. omniscient  C. characterless  D. infinite

19. The Islamic leader of prayer in a mosque is a(n)

    A. mullah  B. adhan  C. imam  D. caliph

20. The Islamic *aqida* is the

    A. spiritual struggle for evil in oneself
    B. Muslim worship service
    C. body of religious and spiritual scholars
    D. profession of faith in the unity of God and the prophethood of Muhammad

21. The New Testament book describing Christian history is

    A. Thessalonians            B. Corinthians
    C. The Gospel               D. Acts of the Apostles

22. The prayer which is said in the morning and the evening in Jewish homes is the

    A. kaddish      B. shema      C. tallith      D. seder

23. A Jain monk will often wear a mask over his mouth. This practice is a manifestation of

    A. the need for anonymity and depersonalization
    B. the desire for absolute purity
    C. enforced fasting
    D. the doctrine of avoiding injury to all forms of life

24. The first Christian proponent of the ontological argument for the existence of God was

    A. St. Thomas Aquinas       B. St. Anselm
    C. St. Augustine            D. Descartes

25. The first great spokesman for the Zen tradition of Japanese Buddhism was

    A. Shinran      B. Nicheren      C. Jodo      D. Eisai

26. Which of the following do NOT comprise a Hindu yoga *chakra*
    The

    A. genitals     B. navel     C. knees     D. throat

27. Which of the following is an Algonquin term for the supernatural world?

    A. Windigo     B. Midewiwin     C. Heyoka     D. Manitou

28. In Hinduism, a *bhuta* is

    A. one who denies the authority of the revelation of the Veda
    B. a malignant spirit
    C. a virtuous woman
    D. an honorific title appended to the name of a learned brahmin

29. The Zoroastrian daily book of prayers is the

    A. Visparat                 B. Khorde Avesta
    C. Videvdat                 D. Yasna

30. The doctrine which has historically done the most to alienate Calvinism from other Christian sects is that of

    A. the predestination of the elect to salvation and the non-elect to damnation
    B. the exaltation of faith and the divine initiative in the process of human salvation
    C. an emphasis on good works
    D. the Bible as the supreme authority of Christians

31. Which of the following terms is used to denote the ancient devotion to gods of the earth, as opposed to those of the sky or heaven?

    A. Chthonian     B. Coptic     C. Orbular     D. Terratheistic

32. In the Jewish tradition, the main difference between the Ashkenazim and Sephardim can best be described as one of

    A. politics     B. theology     C. practice     D. geography

33. The Hebrew Old Testament consists of each of the following parts EXCEPT

    A. Wisdom     B. Prophets     C. Writings     D. Torah

34. Which of the following is NOT a god mentioned in the Vedas?

    A. Indra     B. Agni     C. Brahma     D. Varuna

35. In Islam, the call to prayers at dawn, midday, afternoon, sunset, and dark is the

    A. fatiha     B. salat     C. hanif     D. adhan

36. The most significant contribution of Sikhism's fifth guru, Arjun Dev, was to

    A. compile the Sikh scriptures into the *Adi Granth*
    B. repel the Mughal invaders from the Punjab
    C. emphasize a priority on good works in religious practice
    D. establish the military defense group, the Khalsa

37. Both Hinduism and Buddhism use a gesture of encouragement performed by raising the right hand with the palm extended toward the recipient. This gesture is the

    A. ziyara     B. kshatriya     C. vamsa     D. abhaya

38. Which of the following is one of the two main forms of Mahayana Buddhist thought?

    A. Yogacara          B. Asanga
    C. Sarvastivada      D. Vijnanivada

39. Of the following, the most recently developed religious tradition is

    A. Mormonism          B. Baha'i
    C. Christian Science  D. Sikhism

40. In the Christian tradition, the day of the Last Supper and the day Jesus washed the feet of his disciples are celebrated on

    A. Ash Wednesday      B. Holy Thursday
    C. Maundy Thursday    D. Good Friday

41. Which of the following was a medieval Hindu scholar who claimed the existence of one eternal Being, with no separate souls or eternal selves possessed by different living beings?

    A. Ramakrishna    B. Shankara    C. Ramanuja    D. Madhva

42. Which of the following is a term for pre-Buddhist rites and beliefs?

    A. Bon    B. Shambhala    C. Gesar    D. Bhadu

43. Which of the following are principles of the Augustinian movement of Christian thought?
    I. Evil is the lack of good.
    II. It is the purposes and not the character of its adherents that make the Church holy.
    III. By heredity, humans are tainted by sin.
    IV. One's destiny in heaven or hell is determined by works performed in earthly life.

    The CORRECT answer is:

    A. I, II, III    B. II only    C. III, IV    D. I, IV

44. The first chapter of the Qu'ran, used as a prayer on many occasions, is the

    A. Umma    B. Fatiha    C. Mahdi    D. Hadith

45. What is the term for the theory of understanding or interpreting biblical, philosophical, and literary texts?

    A. Ontology    B. Hermeneutics    C. Ephemera    D. Dogma

46. In Indian thought, what is the term used to denote the wrong, the vicious, the unnatural, or the evil?

    A. Moksha    B. Padartha    C. Adharma    D. Samsara

47. The Sanskrit word which indicates *God* in the general sense for Hindus is

    A. Imayana    B. Krishna    C. Brahma    D. Ishvara

48. Which of the following terms is used to refer to a student of a Hindu guru?

    A. Brahmin    B. Sadhu    C. Chela    D. Acolyte

49. Which of the following is a way in which Islam differs most clearly from Buddhism, Christianity, and Judaism?

    A. Its practitioners are aggressive in their search for converts.
    B. It sees people of other faiths as infidels.
    C. It developed almost entirely in response to a single historical event.
    D. It has remained consistently strong in its homeland since its birth.

50. The most widespread and important of the heterodox students of Christ in the early Church, who held that Christ was not divine but a creation of God, were the    50.____

    A. Homoeans    B. Ninians    C. Arians    D. Anomoeans

## KEY (CORRECT ANSWERS)

| | | | | |
|---|---|---|---|---|
| 1. C | 11. D | 21. D | 31. A | 41. B |
| 2. C | 12. A | 22. B | 32. D | 42. A |
| 3. A | 13. A | 23. D | 33. A | 43. A |
| 4. D | 14. C | 24. B | 34. C | 44. B |
| 5. B | 15. B | 25. D | 35. D | 45. B |
| 6. D | 16. B | 26. C | 36. A | 46. C |
| 7. B | 17. B | 27. D | 37. D | 47. D |
| 8. B | 18. A | 28. B | 38. A | 48. C |
| 9. C | 19. C | 29. B | 39. C | 49. D |
| 10. B | 20. D | 30. A | 40. C | 50. C |

# TEST 3

DIRECTIONS: Each question or incomplete statement is followed by several suggested answers or completions. Select the one that BEST answers the question or completes the statement. *PRINT THE LETTER OF THE CORRECT ANSWER IN THE SPACE AT THE RIGHT.*

1. Which of the following is NOT a modern Zoroastrian sect?　　　　1.____

    A.  Qadimi　　　B.  Mani　　　C.  Falsi　　　D.  Shenshahi

2. Among modern Parsis, a high priest is known as a(n)　　　　2.____

    A.  panthak　　　B.  mobad　　　C.  dastur　　　D.  magus

3. Most of Hinduism's orthodox mythology is based on the　　　　3.____

    A.  dharmasastras　　　B.  Upanishads
    C.  puranas　　　D.  Vedas

4. The name traditionally given to a Christian feast commemorating the purification of Mary and the presentation of Jesus in the Temple, forty days after his birth, is　　　　4.____

    A.  Antiphon　　　B.  Michaelmas
    C.  Assumption　　　D.  Candlemas

5. According to Christian Scientists, Christ was able to transcend himself into the kingdom of heaven by　　　　5.____

    A.  breaking the bounds of ordinary sense perception in the material world
    B.  carrying out his preordained function as an incarnation of God on earth
    C.  performing a prescribed number of good works
    D.  functioning as a consummate healer

6. Each of the following sects descended from the radical 16th-century Anabaptists EXCEPT the　　　　6.____

    A.  Melchiorites　　　B.  Mennonites
    C.  Hutterites　　　D.  Amish

7. Which of the following is NOT a typical Jewish Shabbat ritual?　　　　7.____

    A.  The havdalah
    B.  The shema
    C.  The kiddush
    D.  Lighting at least two candles by the woman of the house before sundown on Friday

8. What is the term for a Jewish prayer book?　　　　8.____

    A.  Tefellin　　　B.  Mezuzah　　　C.  Tallith　　　D.  Siddur

9. Zen can be described as a mingling of each of the following:
   I. Buddhism
   II. Confucianism
   III. Taoism
   IV. Shinto

   The CORRECT answer is:

   A. I, III
   B. I, II, IV
   C. II, III, IV
   D. I, II, III, IV

10. _____ Shinto is the *nationalist* sect of Shinto.

    A. Mountain
    B. Purification
    C. Confucian
    D. Pure

11. The Old Testament story of Cain and Abel almost certainly arose out of a historical conflict between

    A. the Jews who fled Egypt and those who remained behind
    B. the peasant class and the nomadic herdsmen
    C. followers of Moses and those who clung to pagan customs
    D. landowners and peasants

12. The earliest sacred literature of Jainism was embodied in unwritten, memorized verses or lines known as the

    A. Agamas    B. Purvas    C. Siddhas    D. Bastis

13. Which of the following Christian orders does NOT include friars?

    A. Dominicans
    B. Franciscans
    C. Benedictines
    D. Carmelites

14. The fundamental text of the Vedanta philosophy of Hinduism is the

    A. Brahma-Sutra
    B. Upanishads
    C. puranas
    D. Bhagavad Gita

15. The giving of alms, one of the five pillars of Islam, is called by the term

    A. sawm    B. salat    C. zakat    D. haj

16. Which of the following best expresses the underlying principle of Jainism?

    A. Self-denial is the only way to achieve enlightenment.
    B. All of one's actions have a consequence in both this world and the next.
    C. There is only one supreme and all-powerful God, who requires total devotion and obedience.
    D. All living things have an immortal soul that should strive to be liberated from matter.

17. Which of the following is a popular Catholic devotion consisting of the recital of three Ave Marias, each preceded by a versicle and response?

    A. Te Deum
    B. Vespers
    C. The Sanctus
    D. The Angelus

18. The Five Vices of Sikhism include each of the following EXCEPT

    A. attachment to material goods
    B. sloth
    C. anger
    D. lust

19. Which of the following is a Christian term for a manifestation of God, as through events such as fire or thunder?

    A. Theophany
    B. Avatar
    C. Transfiguration
    D. Transsubstantiation

20. In the Buddhist tradition, the practical guide to enlightenment is provided by the

    A. Three Jewels
    B. trikaya
    C. Eightfold Path
    D. Four Noble Truths

21. Which of the following is a Muslim festival devoted to forgiveness?

    A. Lailat-ul-Badar
    B. Id al-fitr
    C. Lailat-ul-Bara'h
    D. Salam Alaikum

22. Which of the following offers the best definition of the term *doctrine*?

    A. The rational analysis of a religious faith
    B. An attempt to give system, clarity, and intellectual power to what is revealed through the mythological and symbolic language of religious faith
    C. The belief in a superhuman controlling power, especially in a personal God or gods entitled to obedience and worship
    D. A means of enacting, in a concrete series of ceremonies or observances, the basic principles of a religion

23. According to the Judeo-Christian tradition, the remedy for the *accidie* sometimes suffered by monks and nuns is

    A. perseverance in prayer
    B. a period of penitent abstinence
    C. pilgrimage
    D. symbolic mortification before God

24. Each of the following religious traditions is today in a period of decline EXCEPT

    A. Zoroastrianism
    B. Sikhism
    C. Taoism
    D. Jainism

25. Which of the following is a Hindu avatar?

    A. Saraswati    B. Ganesha    C. Shiva    D. Krishna

26. The main reason that few of Africa's religions have expanded beyond the realm of their origins is that

    A. Africa has been relatively isolated both socially and geographically
    B. they have little theological or doctrinal elaboration
    C. there was little interaction between tribes of differing religions
    D. they have been perpetually suppressed by conquering people

27. Which of the following is a term for a Roman Catholic liturgical book consisting of psalms, lessons, prayers, and hymns?

    A. Psalter    B. Missal    C. Epistle    D. Breviary

28. The Mahayana school of Buddhism tends to equate nirvana and

    A. samsara    B. shakti    C. moksha    D. bhakti

29. What is the term for the Islamic group who believes that successors to the caliphate should only be men who are descended directly from Muhammad's daughter, Fatima?

    A. Companions  
    B. Unmayads  
    C. Legitimists  
    D. Seveners

30. The spiritual ignorance that is the cause of much suffering in the Hindu tradition is known as

    A. mandir    B. avidya    C. ishvara    D. abhakti

31. The universal elements of Africa's Bantu religion include
    I. a great concern for ancestral spirits
    II. a belief in one supreme god
    III. concern and preparation for the afterlife
    IV. fear of witchcraft

    The CORRECT answer is:

    A. I, II, IV    B. I, III    C. II only    D. III only

32. A Hindu man recognized for his learning and wisdom, who might be consulted and function much as a Jewish rabbi, is a

    A. pujari    B. sadhu    C. pandit    D. guru

33. Which of the following offers the best explanation of the ultimate goal of the Baha'i religion?
    The

    A. performance of good works to invoke God's favor  
    B. ascendance into heaven  
    C. preparation of the faithful for the arrival of the new Bab, or messiah  
    D. establishment and perpetuation of peace

34. What is the collective term for the public prayers, psalms, hymns, and readings of the Roman Catholic Church?

    A. Divine office    B. Canon    C. Liturgy    D. Vestment

35. The lowest of the traditional Hindu castes are the

    A. Vaisya    B. Brahamana    C. Sudra    D. Kshatriya

36. The Qu'ran teaching of *purdah* requires that

    A. strict dietary laws must be observed by the faithful
    B. women must keep the bodies covered and let only their hands and faces show in public
    C. the faithful must fight against the enemies of Islam
    D. Muslims make a pilgrimage to Mecca at least once in their lives

37. In Hinduism, the general term for the female personification of power is

    A. Shakti  B. Parvati  C. Kali  D. Bhakti

38. The *nyaya* school of Hindu thought is mainly devoted to

    A. a theory of atomism
    B. the achievement of disentanglement from world affairs
    C. an investigation and listing of logical arguments
    D. the metaphysical environment necessary for liberation

39. If food has been judged fit to eat by Islamic law, it is described as

    A. zakat  B. halal  C. hijra  D. ka'ba

40. The biblical authority for the Christian Church's requirement of celibacy for clergy is most often traced to

    A. Luke  B. Matthew  C. Paul  D. Romans

41. What is the term for the Islamic call for Allah's blessing?

    A. Al-rahim  B. Bismalah  C. Kalam  D. Fatiha

42. The Buddhist doctrine of *bardo* refers to the

    A. intermediate state between death and rebirth
    B. refusal to do harm of any sort to living creatures
    C. earthly life of a person
    D. persistence in seeking liberation from the cycle of death and rebirth

43. Which of the following texts did the most to promote the Hindu virtue of non-violence, or *ahimsa*?
    The

    A. Bhagavad Gita      B. Atharvaveda
    C. Upanishads         D. puranas

44. In the Roman Catholic Church, ecclesiastical law is also known as _____ law.

    A. evangelical        B. catechismic
    C. synodic            D. canon

45. Which of the following is a term used by anthropoligists to denote a hidden or secret impersonal force which operates silently and invisibly on things and persons?

    A. Mana  B. Totem  C. Deus  D. Anima

46. The _____ comprises the teachings of the founding Guru of Sikhism.

   A. Ragas   B. Panth   C. Japji   D. Rahit

47. According to many scholars, it is likely that Jewish monotheism would not have achieved any importance in the ancient world and would have remained a largely tribal religion, had it not been for the

   A. Diaspora
   B. life of Jesus and the subsequent spread of Christianity
   C. discover of the book of *Deuteronomy*
   D. exodus of the Jews with Moses from Egypt

48. According to the angelology of Dionysius, which of the following does NOT inhabit the top hierarchy of angels?

   A. Throne   B. Cherubim   C. Archangel   D. Seraphim

49. The heart of Buddhist teaching could best be described as

   A. mythological   B. ritualistic
   C. symbolic       D. doctrinal

50. The first day of Lent in the Christian tradition is marked by

   A. Ash Wednesday        B. Holy Thursday
   C. Good Friday          D. Palm Sunday

# KEY (CORRECT ANSWERS)

| | | | | |
|---|---|---|---|---|
| 1. B | 11. B | 21. C | 31. A | 41. B |
| 2. C | 12. B | 22. B | 32. C | 42. A |
| 3. B | 13. C | 23. A | 33. D | 43. C |
| 4. D | 14. A | 24. B | 34. A | 44. D |
| 5. A | 15. C | 25. D | 35. C | 45. A |
| 6. D | 16. D | 26. B | 36. B | 46. C |
| 7. B | 17. D | 27. D | 37. A | 47. B |
| 8. D | 18. B | 28. A | 38. C | 48. C |
| 9. D | 19. A | 29. C | 39. B | 49. D |
| 10. D | 20. C | 30. B | 40. C | 50. A |

# TEST 4

DIRECTIONS: Each question or incomplete statement is followed by several suggested answers or completions. Select the one that BEST answers the question or completes the statement. *PRINT THE LETTER OF THE CORRECT ANSWER IN THE SPACE AT THE RIGHT.*

1. Which of the following was a *Greater Vehicle* Buddhist philosopher who applied the doctrine of impermanence to states?  1.____

    A. Goteshwara  
    B. Nagarjuna  
    C. Shankara  
    D. San Lung Tsung

2. Which of the following is a Jewish festival commemorating the reception of the Ten Commandments by Moses?  2.____

    A. The Day of Atonement  
    B. The Feast of Unleavened Bread  
    C. Sukkoth  
    D. Simchas Torah

3. If the philosophy of Marxism is to be denied as a true religion, it is because it lacks the all-important _____ aspect that links humans to the possibility of an invisible world.  3.____

    A. experiential    B. doctrinal    C. moral    D. social

4. In matters of medical concern, Buddhists generally follow the teachings of the ancient Indian literature comprising the body of Hindu medical lore. What is the name of this text?  4.____

    A. *Rigveda*    B. *Ayruveda*    C. *Samaveda*    D. *Atharvaveda*

5. Each of the following is one of the New Testament's *catholic* epistles EXCEPT  5.____

    A. James    B. Romans    C. II Peter    D. Jude

6. In traditional Indian society, the lower-caste person must avoid coming close to a member of the highest caste.  
   This is an example of  6.____

    A. karma    B. totemism    C. veneration    D. taboo

7. The great world religions each arose from one of three locations in the world: the Middle East, India, and China.  
   The main reason for this is that they  7.____

    A. were probably the most heavily populated areas of the world during the time the religions developed
    B. were probably the locations of the world's first centralized and organized civilizations
    C. were relatively stable, isolated, and homogeneous populations that could sustain the growth of one single and unified body of religious thought
    D. were exceedingly fertile agricultural areas that were heavily dependent upon the forces of nature

8. The oldest of the four schools of Hinayana Buddhism is

   A. Sautrantika    B. Vaibhasika    C. Theravada    D. Sarvastivada

9. What is the term for the Greek translation of the entire Hebrew Bible?

   A. Septuagint    B. Targum    C. Pentateuch    D. Mysteria

10. The *vedanta* school of Hindu thought focuses on

    A. the complexities of Vedic ritual
    B. the relationship between the eternal self and the divine Absolute
    C. liberation from the death/rebirth cycle
    D. the nature of evil

11. What is the term for a Christian book containing lessons from the Bible to be read at services?

    A. Lectionary    B. Breviary    C. Corporal    D. Missal

12. *Siyam,* in the Islamic tradition, refers to

    A. a mat or carpet laid to face Mecca and kneeled on to conduct prayers
    B. the requirement to fast during Ramadan
    C. a common Muslim greeting
    D. the giving of alms

13. By what name is the Jewish festival of Passover, commemorating the flight of the Jews from Egypt, also known?

    A. Haggadah    B. Pesach    C. Shabbat    D. Pentateuch

14. The relative rivival of both Hinduism and Buddhism over the last two centuries can most clearly be attributed to

    A. the rediscovery of the past by people long dominated by European powers
    B. a strong missionary tradition
    C. a population explosion throughout India and East Asia
    D. the migration of practitioners to other parts of the world

15. Which of the following is generally regarded as the founder of Hasidism?

    A. Baal Shem Tov           B. Isaac Luria
    C. Solomon Schechter       D. Abraham Geiger

16. In the _____ religion, the great teachers of the past are referred to as *Tirthankaras* or *Ford-makers.*

    A. Jain    B. Zoroastrian    C. Baha'i    D. Sikh

17. The prayers that must be recited by a Muslim five times a day, to satisfy one of the five pillars of Islam, are the

    A. Sunnah    B. Shema    C. Salat    D. Siyam

18. The Wei-shih school of Chinese Buddhism

    A. was known as the *Discipline* school
    B. is realistic and looks back to the late Lesser Vehicle scriptures
    C. was later to be developed and adapted in Japan
    D. has its origins in Indian idealism

19. In a strict Christian tradition, prayers that should be recited at certain times of the day are referred to as

    A. benefices    B. vespers
    C. orders       D. canonical hours

20. The body of laws in the *Torah* and the *Talmud* are known collectively as the

    A. Kippur    B. Mishnah    C. Halakhah    D. Midrash

21. Which of the following beliefs is/are elements of Jainism?
    I. There is no god.
    II. The universe has no beginning or end.
    III. All living things have an immortal soul.
    IV. Time is a wheel divided into revolving periods of good and bad fortune for humanity.

    The CORRECT answer is:

    A. I, II         B. II *only*
    C. II, III, IV   D. I, II, III, IV

22. The ancient ritual practice of *harakiri*, practiced by Japanese warrior devotees of Shinto, was a part of the code known as

    A. Kami    B. Hachiman    C. Bushido    D. Inari

23. The world's oldest ascetic religious tradition is

    A. Buddhism    B. Jainism
    C. Hinduism    D. Zoroastrianism

24. The term *dukkha* represents the Buddhist belief that

    A. one's fate is determined largely by one's behavior earlier in life
    B. everything eventually leads to suffering
    C. god can only be known through love and devotion
    D. one must fulfill one's given social and moral obligations

25. Which of the following is generally least important to practitioners of Shinto?

    A. Good works    B. Purity
    C. Loyalty       D. Ritual

26. In Indian thought, the soul or essential self is denoted by the term

    A. brahmin    B. sati    C. atman    D. sruti

27. The main difference between Zoroastrianism and the other regional religions of the time was that it

    A. placed an emphasis on ancestor worship
    B. viewed humanity as a constant struggle between good and evil
    C. introduced the concept of free will
    D. placed one supreme god above all others

28. What is the term for a Christian song or chant that is nonmetrical and whose words are taken from Biblical text?

    A. Canticle    B. Plainsong    C. Angelus    D. Evensong

29. The scriptures of _____ are written in the language of Pali, a later derivative of Sanskrit.

    A. Coptic Christianity    B. Zoroastrianism
    C. Jainism                D. Theravada Buddhism

30. Which of the following is a Buddhist festival?

    A. Zazan    B. Agama    C. Punna    D. Wesak

31. The relative modern decline in Christian belief in the West can be traced to the
    I. growth of religious skepticism among the educated classes
    II. Industrial Revolution's disruption of traditional social patterns
    III. fragmentation of the Church into numerous different sects
    IV. lack of state involvement in support of Christian institutions
    The CORRECT answer is:

    A. I, II    B. I, III, IV    C. III, IV    D. II only

32. The *Bhagavad Gita* is a philosophical poem that appears in which of the following Hindu texts?
    The

    A. Ramayana    B. Mhabharata    C. Atharvaveda    D. Upanishads

33. Who is the Hindu god of rain, thunder, and war?

    A. Indra    B. Kalki    C. Hanuman    D. Shiva

34. Every doorpost of a Jewish home should contain a scroll with passages from the Hebrew Bible. The name for this scroll is a

    A. tallith    B. nashim    C. sefirah    D. mezuzah

35. The most common form of asceticism across cultures appears to be

    A. fasting and dietary restrictions    B. sexual continence or celibacy
    C. poverty                             D. seclusion

36. The principle scriptures of the Zoroastrian religion are the

    A. Panths    B. Daxma    C. Avesta    D. Yasna

37. The _____ is a practice associated with the Baha'i religion.

    A. use of professional priests to perform services
    B. existence of sacred religious scriptures
    C. maintenance of a monastic order
    D. performance of complex ceremonial rituals

38. In the mass of the Roman Catholic Church, what is the name for the short prayer that is read before the reading of the epistle?

    A. Anaphora    B. Homily    C. Liturgy    D. Collect

39. Which of the following best describes the relationship between Buddhism and gods?

    A. Buddhism denies the existence of other worldly gods.
    B. It believes that gods may be invoked to assist in one's quest for enlightenment.
    C. Buddhism transcends the worship of gods but does not deny their existence.
    D. It views gods as the all-knowing holders of spiritual power, who are capable of imparting the secrets of existence to people.

40. A Muslim scholar who interprets Islamic law is a(n)

    A. jinn    B. caliph    C. mullah    D. imam

41. Which of the following is NOT an avatar according to the Hindu tradition?

    A. Krishna    B. Vishnu    C. Rama    D. Buddha

42. The Cabbalistic tradition of Judaism includes each of the following notions EXCEPT

    A. a de-emphasis of the Temple cult and a shift toward a religion of the home and synagogue
    B. the doctrine of the spheres, mediating between the infinate light and the created universe
    C. a recognition of angels and other such beings that act as communicators between God and man
    D. an androgynous forerunner of humanity

43. Which of the following is a Sikh sect that practices asceticism?

    A. Sahajdharas    B. Nirankari
    C. Udasis         D. Singhs

44. What is the term for a Christian prayer that is directed through the Virgin Mary?

    A. Plainsong    B. Vesper    C. Madonna    D. Rosary

45. The *mimamsa* school of Hindu thought began as a(n)

    A. inventory of logical arguments
    B. attempt to organize the principles of interpretation of the Vedic scriptures
    C. practical guide to enlightenment
    D. attempt to articulate the single Creator, Brahma

46. Probably the largest denominational group in Protestantism today are the

    A. Episcopalians          B. Methodists
    C. Presbyterians          D. Baptists

47. What is the Hebrew name of God used in the Torah?

    A. Jehovah     B. Adonai     C. Elohim     D. Yahweh

48. In most Indian schools of thought, the key to one's salvation is essentially

    A. charity               B. knowledge
    C. love                  D. faith

49. In the Christian tradition, what is the theological term for the desire for the forbidden?

    A. Lasciviousness        B. Wantonness
    C. Debauchery            D. Concupiscence

50. According to the Companions, the caliph of Islam should be

    A. chosen directly by the leaders
    B. dictated by the preceding caliph
    C. drawn from their number in some form of election
    D. determined by heredity, through descendants of Muhammad's daughter, Fatima

# KEY (CORRECT ANSWERS)

| | | | | |
|---|---|---|---|---|
| 1. B | 11. A | 21. D | 31. A | 41. D |
| 2. D | 12. B | 22. C | 32. B | 42. A |
| 3. A | 13. B | 23. B | 33. A | 43. B |
| 4. B | 14. A | 24. B | 34. D | 44. D |
| 5. B | 15. A | 25. A | 35. A | 45. B |
| 6. D | 16. A | 26. C | 36. C | 46. D |
| 7. B | 17. C | 27. D | 37. B | 47. C |
| 8. C | 18. D | 28. A | 38. D | 48. B |
| 9. A | 19. D | 29. D | 39. C | 49. D |
| 10. B | 20. C | 30. D | 40. C | 50. C |

# EXAMINATION SECTION
# TEST 1

DIRECTIONS: Each question or incomplete statement is followed by several suggested answers or completions. Select the one that BEST answers the question or completes the statement. *PRINT THE LETTER OF THE CORRECT ANSWER IN THE SPACE AT THE RIGHT.*

1. Ninevah was  1._____

    A. the largest city during Jonah's life
    B. capital of Assyria
    C. capital of Babylon
    D. A and C
    E. A and B

2. Isaiah was known as  2._____

    A. a judge
    B. the weeping prophet
    C. the Messianic prophet
    D. a Gentile spokesman
    E. a king's aide

3. Ruth was a Moabitish woman who  3._____

    A. married Moses
    B. gave up her gods for Jehovah
    C. became queen after Vashti
    D. was known as a harlot
    E. never married

4. Proverbs was written by  4._____

    A. David    B. Samuel    C. Moses
    D. Solomon    E. Jeremiah

5. Melchizedeck was  5._____

    A. the first priest
    B. King of Siam
    C. tithe payer to Abraham
    D. ashamed of his lineage
    E. born near the time of David

6. The FIRST king of Israel was  6._____

    A. Solomon    B. David    C. Samuel    D. Saul    E. Samson

7. Samson was judge of Israel even though he  7._____

    A. married an Egyptian
    B. killed 1,000 men on one occasion
    C. burned half of Rome
    D. caught 300 wild bears
    E. lived in the little town of Hebron

103

8. Joshua was    8.___

    A. the successor of Caleb
    B. one of the twelve spies of the Philistines
    C. one adult over twenty years old who entered the Canaan land
    D. the writer of the Pentateuch
    E. a general under King Saul

9. Solomon was    9.___

    A. David's son by Bathsheba
    B. the second King of Israel
    C. collected all the materials to build the temple
    D. reigned for 51 years
    E. a contemporary of Isaiah

10. Elijah    10.___

    A. succeeded Elisha
    B. slew 400 prophets of Baal
    C. brought a little boy back to life
    D. killed a she bear
    E. lived under a Nazarite vow

11. Moses    11.___

    A. lost his eyesight
    B. led Israel across the Sea of Galilee
    C. married an Amorite
    D. killed an Egyptian
    E. died at the age of 100

12. The Ten Commandments were    12.___

    A. given at Mount Nebo
    B. kept in the ark of the covenant
    C. written on papyrus paper
    D. were in the Israel Museum until recently
    E. all of the above

13. Abraham    13.___

    A. married his cousin
    B. wrote the code of Hamarobi
    C. was reared at Ninevah
    D. was a pauper
    E. lied

14. Jezebel    14.___

    A. had Naboth executed          B. dogs lapped her blood
    C. tried to enhance Jehovah worship   D. all of the above
    E. A and B

15. Job                                                                                                    15.____

    A. may have been a Gentile
    B. does not fit into the Jewish lineage
    C. seemingly lived before the law of Moses
    D. all of the above
    E. A and B

16. Jeremiah was                                                                                           16.____

    A. the weeping prophet
    B. the father of three prominent boys
    C. alive during the darkest days of Israel
    D. all of the above
    E. A and C

17. David                                                                                                  17.____

    A. committed adultery
    B. bestowed great honor upon Uriah
    C. killed King Saul
    D. installed Absalom as his successor
    E. wrote all of the Psalms

18. Goshen was                                                                                             18.____

    A. a small fertile land near Egypt
    B. where Jacob and his family moved from
    C. where Jacob lived when he died
    D. all of the above
    E. A and C

19. Caleb was                                                                                              19.____

    A. a coward                              B. a faithful spy
    C. Moses' successor                      D. all of the above
    E. none of the above

20. Moses                                                                                                  20.____

    A. lived in Midian 42 years
    B. was reared as a shepherd boy
    C. lead Israel across the Sea of Galilee
    D. received the law on Mount Nebo
    E. none of the above

21. Absalom                                                                                                21.____

    A. married his sister Tamar
    B. had long red hair
    C. was a faithful servant to David
    D. tried to oust Solomon as the new king
    E. gave full support to Solomon as the new ruler of Israel

22. Saul sinned against God in that he                                                    22.___

    A. committed adultery
    B. worshipped idols
    C. refused to offer sacrifices
    D. slew the prophets
    E. refused to harm Agag

23. The story of Hosea and Gomer is                                                       23.___

    A. a great lesson of forgiveness
    B. about two kings
    C. a plot of revenge
    D. about the Assyrian captivity
    E. none of the above

24. The first judge in Israel was                                                          24.___

    A. Samuel            B. Othniel           C. Enud
    D. Samson            E. Gideon

25. Elijah announced Ahab's doom because he                                                25.___

    A. worshipped Baal
    B. had stolen Naboth's vineyard
    C. had sought to kill Elijah
    D. had formed an alliance with heathens
    E. refused to pray

26. Esther became the wife of                                                              26.___

    A. Baruch            B. Mordecai          C. Haggai
    D. Ahasuerus         E. Haman

27. The Persian king who FIRST commanded the temple to be restored was                    27.___

    A. Cyrus             B. Darius            C. Nebuchadnezzar
    D. Alexander         E. Artaxerxes

28. Jeroboam was the                                                                       28.___

    A. son of Solomon              B. son of David
    C. son of Jonathan             D. servant of Solomon
    E. servant of David

29. Moses is *now* accepted as the author of the first five books because                 29.___

    A. writing predates Moses
    B. the Jews and Christians always accepted this
    C. internal evidence supports his authorship
    D. Jesus attributed this work to him
    E. all of the above

30. God made a promise to Abraham that He would        30._____

    A. make of him a great nation
    B. bless those who blessed him
    C. see the promise before his death
    D. all of the above
    E. A and B

31. Prophecy about Rebekah's twin boys *before* they were born was        31._____

    A. two nations are in thy womb
    B. they will both be kings
    C. the elder will serve the younger
    D. all of the above
    E. A and C

32. Simeon and Levi rewarded a whole city of men for raping their sister Dinah by        32._____

    A. pouting
    B. stealing some food
    C. burning their courthouse
    D. forgiving them
    E. killing them

33. These crimes carried capital punishment:        33._____

    A. murder                          B. striking your parent
    C. stealing or kidnapping          D. all of the above
    E. A and C

34. God allowed the poor to offer these as a substitute for a lamb:        34._____

    A. Two turtledoves
    B. Two young pigeons
    C. Two quarts of unleavened bread
    D. A and B
    E. None of the above

35. Nadab and Abihu were punished because they        35._____

    A. ate fat meat
    B. stole some pagan gods
    C. refused to tell the truth
    D. offered unholy or strange fire to God
    E. touched the ark of the covenant

36. The atonement sacrifice was performed by        36._____

    A. offering one goat
    B. loosing the other goat
    C. sprinkling blood on the second goat and turning it loose in the wilderness
    D. all of the above
    E. A and B

37. The Hebrews were to remember the poor by

    A. not stripping the vines or picking the second crop
    B. letting them pilfer their storehouse
    C. allowing them to come to the back door and beg
    D. all of the above
    E. none of the above

38. Levites were forbidden to be priests if they

    A. were deaf
    B. were blind or lame
    C. had a limb too long or injured foot or hand
    D. all of the above
    E. A and B

39. On the Sabbath year,

    A. all slaves were freed
    B. all land was returned to its original owner
    C. the land rested
    D. all of the above
    E. none of the above

40. Korah helped lead a rebellion against Moses and

    A. the earth opened up and swallowed all the rebels
    B. the rebels all were stricken with tumors
    C. Moses almost lost his faith
    D. he was publicly stoned
    E. he and all his followers were stoned

41. Miriam rebuked Moses for marrying a dark woman and

    A. Miriam was stricken with tumors
    B. Mirian was stricken with leprosy
    C. Moses divorced his wife
    D. all of the above
    E. none of the above

42. The man who gathered sticks on the Sabbath was

    A. driven out of the camp      B. fined with one lamb
    C. stoned                       D. all of the above
    E. none of the above

43. When Balaam tried to curse Israel for a bribe,

    A. his donkey spoke             B. he stuttered
    C. was stricken dumb            D. all of the above
    E. none of the above

44. To walk in the ways of Jeroboam meant to    44._____

    A. be a brave man      B. be a coward
    C. worship idols      D. worship Jehovah
    E. be a man about town

45. King Saul was    45._____

    A. short
    B. first king of the divided Israel
    C. very aggressive when he was chosen to be king
    D. a personal friend of Abraham
    E. none of the above

46. Uzzah was slain because he    46._____

    A. tripped in battle
    B. touched the Ark of the Covenant
    C. raped Dinah, Jacob's daughter
    D. stole Lamech's gods
    E. all of the above

47. David's reign was marked by    47._____

    A. impatience      B. justice and equality
    C. harshness      D. lack of vision
    E. none of the above

48. God divided Israel because of Solomon's    48._____

    A. worshipping of idols
    B. marrying so many wives
    C. not killing King Agag
    D. playing the role of a priest
    E. executing Uriah, an innocent man

49. The shadow on the dial of Ahaz returned 10 degrees in order to Hezekiah that he would    49._____

    A. live 15 more years
    B. win the great battle of Jericho
    C. die in battle
    D. be the next King of Israel
    E. none of the above

50. Haman, who hated Mordecai, *finally* ended up being    50._____

    A. stoned      B. crucified      C. hanged
    D. scourged      E. exiled

## KEY (CORRECT ANSWERS)

| | | | | |
|---|---|---|---|---|
| 1. E | 11. D | 21. B | 31. E | 41. B |
| 2. C | 12. B | 22. E | 32. E | 42. C |
| 3. B | 13. E | 23. A | 33. D | 43. A |
| 4. D | 14. E | 24. B | 34. D | 44. C |
| 5. A | 15. D | 25. B | 35. D | 45. E |
| 6. D | 16. E | 26. D | 36. D | 46. B |
| 7. B | 17. A | 27. A | 37. A | 47. B |
| 8. C | 18. E | 28. D | 38. D | 48. A |
| 9. A | 19. B | 29. D | 39. C | 49. A |
| 10. B | 20. E | 30. E | 40. A | 50. C |

# TEST 2

DIRECTIONS: Each question or incomplete statement is followed by several suggested answers or completions. Select the one that BEST answers the question or completes the statement. *PRINT THE LETTER OF THE CORRECT ANSWER IN THE SPACE AT THE RIGHT.*

Questions 1-25.

DIRECTIONS: Questions 1 through 25 are True-False. Mark A if the question is True and B if the question is False.

1. Job was forsaken during his time of testing by everyone except his wife.   1.\_\_\_\_
2. The temple was *completely* finished and dedicated by Solomon.   2.\_\_\_\_
3. Solomon remained in favor with the Lord until his death.   3.\_\_\_\_
4. David was prohibited from building the temple because he was a man of war.   4.\_\_\_\_
5. Eli was rebuked because he did not restrain his two sons.   5.\_\_\_\_
6. Saul was killed in battle by the Philistines.   6.\_\_\_\_
7. It took *approximately* 1500 years to write the Old Testament.   7.\_\_\_\_
8. The lineage of Christ is traced back through Cain.   8.\_\_\_\_
9. Lot coined the expression, *Let there be no strife between me and thee because we be brethren.*   9.\_\_\_\_
10. When Lot was captured, Abraham took his own servants and chased after the kings and rescued Lot.   10.\_\_\_\_
11. God made the fleshly covenant of circumcision with Abraham.   11.\_\_\_\_
12. Laban was a kind and honest father-in-law to Jacob.   12.\_\_\_\_
13. Moses *great* sin was killing the Egyptian. This kept him out of the promised land.   13.\_\_\_\_
14. The book of Leviticus deals with the numbering of the people.   14.\_\_\_\_
15. The Levites were given *no* land when Canaan was divided among the twelve tribes.   15.\_\_\_\_
16. A cloud hovered over the tabernacle by day and a pillar of fire by night.   16.\_\_\_\_
17. Deuteronomy means the *Second Law* or a restating of the *First Law.*   17.\_\_\_\_
18. The walls of Jericho fell outward to prove that it was an act of God.   18.\_\_\_\_
19. Though it was *against* the law of the land, Saul consulted a witch at Endor to find out about his future.   19.\_\_\_\_
20. David rewarded the Amalekite with three pieces of gold for claiming to have killed King Saul.   20.\_\_\_\_

21. One young unnamed prophet was killed by a lion because he believed a lie.        21.____

22. The theme of the book of Job is sympathy.        22.____

23. Wisdom is NOT the theme of Proverbs.        23.____

24. There was a strong middle class of people during the time of Isaiah.        24.____

25. For three years, Isaiah walked naked and barefooted as a sign of God's judgment against Egypt and Ethiopia.        25.____

Questions 26-50.

DIRECTIONS: Questions 26 through 50 are identification. Choose the CORRECT answer in each case.

26. *Vanity, vanity, all is vanity:*        26.____
    A. Saul         B. David        C. Solomon
    D. Rehoboam     E. Jeroboam

27. Pouting preacher:        27.____
    A. Hosea        B. Jeremiah     C. Samuel
    D. Jonah        E. Ezekiel

28. *Curse God and die:*        28.____
    A. Jezebel      B. Ahab         C. Saul
    D. Daniel       E. Job's wife

29. Carried his own death note:        29.____
    A. Uriah        B. Benjamin     C. Jonathan
    D. Jeroboam     E. Abel

30. Didn't want to sell Joseph:        30.____
    A. Benjamin     B. Simeon       C. Levi
    D. Reuben       E. God

31. Moses' father-in-law:        31.____
    A. Methuselah   B. Enoch        C. Seth
    D. Tobiah       E. Jethro

32. A mighty hunter:        32.____
    A. Abel         B. Nimrod       C. Seth
    D. Lamech       E. Noah

33. Where the ark rested:        33.____
    A. Nebo         B. Ararat       C. Hermon
    D. Carmel       E. Gerizim

34. Fire consumed Elijah's sacrifice at mount:    34._____
    A. Tabor       B. Gilead       C. Carmel
    D. Hermon      E. Zion

35. Healed of leprosy:    35._____
    A. Mordecai    B. Haman       C. Ahasuerus
    D. Naaman      E. Cyrus

36. Destroyed for sacrilege:    36._____
    A. Nadab       B. Caleb       C. Jephthah
    D. Joshua      E. Abel

37. First bigamist:    37._____
    A. Seth        B. Methuselah  C. Enoch
    D. Cain        E. Lamech

38. Best friend of David:    38._____
    A. Saul        B. Absalom     C. Solomon
    D. Jonathan    E. Uriah

39. Resisted fornication:    39._____
    A. Elijah      B. Moses       C. Ezekiel
    D. Joseph      E. Judah

40. Means laughter:    40._____
    A. Isaac       B. Jacob       C. Esau
    D. Ishmael     E. Abraham

41. Son of a bondwoman:    41._____
    A. Joseph      B. Abraham     C. Ishmael
    D. Isaac       E. Jacob

42. His two daughters bore him sons:    42._____
    A. Reuben      B. Simeon      C. Levi
    D. Jonathan    E. Lot

43. The uncircumcised:    43._____
    A. Samaritans  B. Gentiles    C. Moabites
    D. Jews        E. Romans

44. Hairy and rough:    44._____
    A. Dan         B. Daniel      C. Esau
    D. Jacob       E. Mordecai

45. Called down fire from Heaven:    45._____
    A. Saul        B. Abihu       C. Aaron
    D. Elijah      E. Samuel

46. First to destroy the temple:

    A. Babylon  B. Assyria  C. Persia
    D. Philista  E. Canaan

47. First high priest:

    A. Abraham  B. Aaron  C. Levi
    D. Jacob  E. Joseph

48. Put out the fleece:

    A. Gideon  B. Barak  C. Miriam
    D. Ruth  E. Naomi

49. Anointed David as King:

    A. Saul  B. Eli  C. Elisha
    D. Elijah  E. Samuel

50. Circumcised at age 99:

    A. Moses  B. David  C. Abraham
    D. Jacob  E. Isaac

## KEY (CORRECT ANSWERS)

| | | | | |
|---|---|---|---|---|
| 1. B | 11. A | 21. A | 31. E | 41. C |
| 2. A | 12. B | 22. B | 32. B | 42. E |
| 3. B | 13. B | 23. B | 33. B | 43. B |
| 4. A | 14. B | 24. B | 34. C | 44. C |
| 5. A | 15. A | 25. A | 35. D | 45. D |
| 6. B | 16. A | 26. C | 36. A | 46. A |
| 7. A | 17. A | 27. D | 37. E | 47. B |
| 8. B | 18. A | 28. E | 38. D | 48. A |
| 9. B | 19. A | 29. A | 39. D | 49. E |
| 10. A | 20. B | 30. D | 40. A | 50. C |

# EXAMINATION SECTION
# TEST 1

DIRECTIONS: Below are some proverbs, and you are to indicate what they mean. You are to choose the BEST answer to each proverb; the one which BEST explains what the proverb means. *PRINT THE LETTER OF THE CORRECT ANSWER IN THE SPACE AT THE RIGHT.*

SAMPLE QUESTIONS

    A.  DON'T CROSS THE BRIDGE UNTIL YOU GET TO IT.
        A.  The bridge is a long ways off.
        B.  People won't like you if you are cross.
        C.  Don't worry about troubles until they come.
        D.  Don't be foolish.

The CORRECT answer is C.

    B.  DON'T CRY OVER SPILT MILK.
        A.  It won't do any good to cry.
        B.  Don't be concerned about mistakes of the past.
        C.  Stop crying and clean it up.
        D.  It is better to laugh than to cry.

The CORRECT answer is B.

1. ROME WAS NOT BUILT IN A DAY.

    A.  It takes some things longer to happen than others.
    B.  It took a number of years.
    C.  Great things come about slowly.
    D.  You can't do certain things in a day.

1.\_\_\_\_

2. WHERE THERE'S A WILL THERE'S A WAY.

    A.  There is always a right way to do something.
    B.  If you keep trying, you will succeed.
    C.  There's always a way for everything.
    D.  If one has determination, he will succeed.

2.\_\_\_\_

3. STRIKE WHILE THE IRON IS HOT.

    A.  Be quick and alert.
    B.  Iron with a hot iron, a cold one won't do.
    C.  That's when it bends the best.
    D.  Do something when the time is right.

3.\_\_\_\_

4. RICHES SERVE A WISE MAN BUT COMMAND A FOOL.

    A.  Don't let money go to your head.
    B.  The poor work for the rich.
    C.  Money may help or hinder, according to the individual.
    D.  Don't beg, borrow or steal.

4.\_\_\_\_

5. GREAT BODIES MOVE SLOWLY.

   A. The bigger you are the slower you are.
   B. Large things cannot be moved quickly.
   C. It is better to think about spiritual things than your physical body.
   D. Great things are done little by little.

6. BETTER BE HAPPY THAN WISE.

   A. Wise people are not happy.
   B. Don't let money stand in your way.
   C. Happiness in life is more important than anything.
   D. Happiness is a great feeling.

7. THE SUN SHINES UPON ALL ALIKE.

   A. It's the same sun everywhere.
   B. All are created equal.
   C. The sun shines on everybody.
   D. People that do the same things are alike.

8. DON'T JUDGE A BOOK BY ITS COVER.

   A. There is good inside everything.
   B. Read a book before you judge it.
   C. Don't judge people by looks only.
   D. A nice cover doesn't make good reading.

9. THE MORE COST, THE MORE HONOR.

   A. For honor and society, it costs.
   B. The harder a thing is to get, the more you appreciate it.
   C. The higher the price, the better a thing is.
   D. Good things have to be paid for in some way.

10. DON'T SWAP (TRADE) HORSES WHEN CROSSING A STREAM.

    A. Make up your mind before you do anything.
    B. Don't antagonize animals or people when they are helping you.
    C. Don't change ideas when something is half done.
    D. Don't try something until you're able to do it.

11. GOLD GOES IN AT ANY GATE EXCEPT HEAVEN'S.

    A. No one can be as good as gold.
    B. Anyone would take money.
    C. Fortune only comes to those who work for it.
    D. You can't buy morals.

12. A DROWNING MAN WILL CLUTCH AT A STRAW.  12.____
    A. When a person is drowning, he'll grab the person nearest to him.
    B. No one will ever actually give up on anything.
    C. A desperate person will try anything.
    D. Don't ever let go.

13. THE WORST SPOKE IN A CART BREAKS FIRST.  13.____
    A. The bad piece breaks first.
    B. Don't speak before you think.
    C. The weakest are always the first to go down.
    D. It takes a good man to keep on trying.

14. THE GRASS IS ALWAYS GREENER IN THE OTHER FELLOW'S YARD.  14.____
    A. He works to keep his looking nice.
    B. Don't stay in one place to do something.
    C. Always live within your means.
    D. Every job looks better than your own.

15. THE WIFE IS THE KEY TO THE HOUSE.  15.____
    A. What she wants, she gets.
    B. She's a partner.
    C. Her efforts make it a home.
    D. Use the key wisely and lovingly.

16. HE WHO STUMBLES TWICE OVER ONE STONE DESERVES TO BREAK HIS SHINS.  16.____
    A. If you're careless, you deserve it.
    B. Once should teach a lesson.
    C. A person should learn by experience.
    D. You should watch where you're walking.

17. LET SLEEPING DOGS LIE.  17.____
    A. Don't stir up old troubles.
    B. Be kind to dumb animals.
    C. Let those who don't wish to learn alone.
    D. Because he might bite.

18. QUICKLY COME, QUICKLY GO. (EASY COME, EASY GO.)  18.____
    A. Always coming and going and never satisfied.
    B. What you get easily does not mean much to you.
    C. Always do things on time.
    D. Most people do as they please and go as they please.

19. BARKING DOGS SELDOM BITE.  19.____
    A. Barking dogs are friendly dogs.
    B. Too busy barking to bite.
    C. Things that make noise seldom are dangerous.
    D. A man who brags isn't likely to live up to it.

20. THE USED KEY IS ALWAYS BRIGHT.   20.____

    A. Something old is better than something new.
    B. The key used the most doesn't grow rusty.
    C. A person who uses his mind a lot becomes very smart.
    D. The person who brags should have a reason.

21. THERE'S MANY A SLIP TWIXT (BETWEEN) THE CUP AND THE LIP.   21.____

    A. Something can happen at the last minute.
    B. Don't talk too much while eating.
    C. A lot can happen between plan and completion.
    D. Don't talk about people too much.

22. A ROLLING STONE GATHERS NO MOSS.   22.____

    A. Be consistent.
    B. The moss gets brushed off.
    C. If you don't settle down you won't accomplish much.
    D. A person who thinks no evil does no evil.

23. ALL IS NOT GOLD THAT GLITTERS.   23.____

    A. Don't let temptation get you.
    B. Other things than gold glitter too.
    C. Everything that looks good isn't necessarily good.
    D. Some things may fool you.

24. THE PROOF OF THE PUDDING IS IN THE EATING.   24.____

    A. Something is good only if it tastes good.
    B. You know pudding by eating it.
    C. You can tell how good a thing is by how well it works.
    D. Things often look good but taste bad.

25. WORDS CUT MORE THAN SWORDS.   25.____

    A. Words always mean more.
    B. A person might lose his temper.
    C. There is nothing as bad as a bad word.
    D. Words can accomplish more than wars.

26. IT NEVER RAINS BUT IT POURS.   26.____

    A. A little is as bad as a lot.
    B. When something goes wrong, everything does.
    C. It always rains hard.
    D. It never suits your fancy.

27. ONE SWALLOW (BIRD) DOESN'T MAKE A SUMMER.   27.____

    A. Because a person thinks so doesn't mean he's right.
    B. It takes all the parts to make a whole.
    C. It takes different things to make up summer.
    D. It takes a long time for time to pass.

28. SPEECH IS THE PICTURE OF THE MIND.                                28._____

    A. To have good speech will always help you.
    B. Words paint pictures in the mind.
    C. Speech can accomplish a lot of things.
    D. You are judged by what you say.

29. ALL'S WELL THAT ENDS WELL.                                        29._____

    A. Anything that is good remains good.
    B. Things usually turn out well in the end.
    C. If something turns out right, the beginning is no longer important.
    D. Don't start something and then not finish it.

30. TOO MANY COOKS SPOIL THE BROTH.                                   30._____

    A. Too many bosses are not good for a job.
    B. One person can do something as well as two.
    C. You'll have too many ideas.
    D. It doesn't take much work to do a little thing.

31. A STREAM CANNOT RISE HIGHER THAN ITS SOURCE.                      31._____

    A. There is no short cut to success.
    B. A person is no better than his background.
    C. Water won't run uphill.
    D. You have a peak in life.

32. DON'T CAST PEARLS BEFORE SWINE (PIGS).                            32._____

    A. Put your efforts where they're appreciated.
    B. Don't give pearls to fools.
    C. Don't be wasteful.
    D. Don't always put yourself before everybody,

33. ONE MAY RIDE A FREE HORSE TO DEATH.                               33._____

    A. Don't take advantage of someone's generosity.
    B. Something free is no good.
    C. Take advantage of what is given you.
    D. Don't take everything free, work for something.

34. WHEN THE CAT'S AWAY, THE MICE WILL PLAY.                          34._____

    A. When authority is gone things will be done that shouldn't be done.
    B. No work and all play is bad.
    C. When one isn't watched, he will play.
    D. When the danger is gone, they will play.

35. DON'T THROW GOOD MONEY AFTER BAD.                                 35._____

    A. Don't gamble with a cheater.
    B. Be wise and think of the future.
    C. When you've lost out in something, accept the fact.
    D. Don't waste your money.

36. A DISEASE KNOWN IS HALF CURED.   36._____

   A. A good doctor can tell what is wrong with you.
   B. You have to understand the problem before you can solve it.
   C. You can only half cure some things.
   D. Diagnosis comes before treatment.

37. A GOLDEN HAMMER BREAKS AN IRON DOOR.   37._____

   A. Virtue conquers all.
   B. You have to use what tools you have to work with.
   C. The stronger a thing is, the harder to break it.
   D. Gold is more powerful than iron.

38. CROOKED LOGS MAKE A STRAIGHT FIRE.   38._____

   A. Even the humblest can create things of beauty.
   B. Handicaps may be used to advantage.
   C. There is some good in everybody.
   D. Things will come out all right in the end.

39. THE GOOD IS THE ENEMY OF THE BEST.   39._____

   A. Get the best of your enemy whenever you can.
   B. It is best to be good even if you fail.
   C. We should love our enemies.
   D. Most people are too easily satisfied.

40. THE HOT COAL BURNS, THE COLD ONE BLACKENS.   40._____

   A. Impetuous action may hurt your reputation.
   B. The burned child avoids the fire.
   C. Extremes of anything are bad.
   D. Leave dangerous things alone.

---

## KEY (CORRECT ANSWERS)

| | | | | | | | |
|---|---|---|---|---|---|---|---|
| 1. | C | 11. | D | 21. | C | 31. | B |
| 2. | D | 12. | C | 22. | C | 32. | A |
| 3. | D | 13. | C | 23. | C | 33. | A |
| 4. | C | 14. | D | 24. | C | 34. | A |
| 5. | D | 15. | C | 25. | D | 35. | C |
| 6. | C | 16. | C | 26. | B | 36. | B |
| 7. | B | 17. | A | 27. | B | 37. | A |
| 8. | C | 18. | B | 28. | D | 38. | B |
| 9. | B | 19. | D | 29. | C | 39. | D |
| 10. | C | 20. | C | 30. | A | 40. | C |

# BIBLICAL QUOTATIONS

## TEN COMMANDMENTS (EXODUS, CH. XX)

1. I am the Lord thy God. Thou shalt have no other gods before me.
2. Thou shalt not make any graven images.
3. Thou shalt not take the name of the Lord thy God in vain.
4. Remember the sabbath day to keep it holy.
5. Honor thy father and thy mother.
6. Thou shalt not kill.
7. Thou shalt not commit adultery.
8. Thou shalt not steal.
9. Thou shalt not bear false witness against thy neighbor.
10. Thou shalt not covet thy neighbor's goods.

## PETER

1. Charity shall cover the multitude of sins.

## JAMES

1. Faith without works is dead.

## HEBREWS

1. Whom the Lord loveth, he chasteneth.
2. Be not forgetful to entertain strangers, for thereby some have entertained angels unawares.

## TIMOTHY

1. We brought nothing into this world, and it is certain we can carry nothing out.
2. The love of money is the root of all evil.

## THESSALONIANS

1. Labor of love.

## GALATEANS

1. Every man shall bear his own burden.
2. Whatsoever a man soweth, that shall he also reap.

## CORINTHIANS

1. Absent in body but present in spirit.
2. A little leaven leaveneth the whole lump.
3. Though I speak with the tongues of men and of angels, and have not charity, I am become as sounding brass or a tinkling cymbal.

4. When I was a child, I spake as a child.... When I became a man, I put away childish things.
5. And now abideth faith, hope, charity, these three; but the greatest of these is charity.
6. O death, where is thy sting? O grave, where is thy victory?
7. Not of the letter but of the spirit; for the letter killeth, but the spirit giveth life.
8. The things which are seen are temporal; but the things which are not seen are eternal.
9. God loveth a cheerful giver.
10. For ye suffer fools gladly, seeing ye yourselves are wise.
11. A thorn in the flesh.

## ROMANS

1. Wherein thou judgest another, thou condemnest thyself.
2. The wages of sin is death.
3. If God be for us, who can be against us?
4. None of us liveth to himself.

## JOHN

1. He that is without sin among you, let him first cast a stone at her.
2. The truth shall make you free.
3. In my Father's house are many mansions.
4. Greater love hath no man than this, that he lay down his life for his friends.
5. It is more blessed to give than to receive.

## MARK

1. If a house be divided against itself, that house cannot stand.
2. Physician, heal thyself.
3. The laborer is worthy of his hire.
4. He that is not with me is against me.

## MATTHEW

1. Ye are the salt of the earth; but if the salt have lost its savor, wherewith shall it be salted?
2. When thou doest alms, let not thy left hand know what thy right hand doeth.
3. Give us this day our daily bread.
4. Lay up for yourselves treasures in heaven.
5. No man can serve two masters.... Ye cannot serve God and Mammon.
6. Consider the lilies of the field, how they grow; they toil not, neither do they spin.
7. Take therefore no thought for the morrow; for the morrow shall take thought for the things of itself. Sufficient unto the day is the evil thereof.
8. Neither cast ye your pearls before swine.
9. Ask and it shall be given you; seek and ye shall find; knock and it shall be opened unto you.
10. Therefore all things whatsoever ye would that men should do to you, do ye even so to them; for this is the law and the prophets.

11. By their fruits ye shall know them.
12. A prophet is not without honor save in his own country and in his own house.
13. If the blind lead the blind, both shall fall into the ditch.
14. Get thee behind me, Satan.
15. What is a man profited, if he shall gain the whole world, and lose his own soul?
16. What therefore God hath joined together, let not man put asunder.
17. Love thy neighbor as thyself.
18. It is easier for a camel to go through the eye of a needle than for a rich man to enter into the kingdom of God.
19. For many are called, but few are chosen.
20. Render therefore unto Caesar the things which are Caesar's.
21. False prophets.
22. Welldone, thou good and faithful servant.
23. Unto him that hath shall be given and he shall have abundance; but from him that hath not, shall be taken away even the little which he hath.
24. Inasmuch as ye have done it unto one of the least of these my brethren, ye have done it unto me.
25. The spirit indeed is willing, but the flesh is weak.
26. All they that take the sword shall perish with the sword.

## DANIEL

1. Thou art weighed in the balance and art found waiting. (Mene, mene, tekel, upharsin)
2. According to the law of the Medes and Persians.
3. They brought Daniel and cast him into the den of lions.

## JEREMIAH

1. Is there no balm in Gilead? Is there no physician there?
2. Can the Ethiopian change his skin or the leopard his spots?

## ISAIAH

1. They shall beat their swords into plowshares, and their spears into pruning hooks; nation shall not lift up sword against nation, neither shall they learn war any more.
2. The wolf also shall dwell with the lamb, and the leopard shall lie down with the kid.
3. Watchman, what of the night?
4. Let us eat and drink; for tomorrow we shall die.
5. We have made a covenant with death, and with hell are we at agreement.
6. The desert shall rejoice, and blossom as the rose.
7. Set thine house in order.
8. All flesh is grass.
9. They shall see eye to eye.
10. We all, like sheep, have gone astray.
11. He is brought as a lamb to the slaughter.
12. I am holier than thou.

## THE SONG OF SOLOMON

1. I am the rose of Sharon and the lily of the valleys.
2. For, lo! the winter is past, the rain is over and gone; the flowers appear on the earth; the time of the singing of the birds is come, and the voice of the turtle is heard in the land.
3. The little foxes that spoil the vines.

## ECCLESIASTES

1. There is no new thing under the sun.
2. He that increaseth knowledge increaseth sorrow.
3. To every thing there is a season, and a time to every purpose under the heaven.
4. It is better to go to the house of mourning than to go to the house of feasting.
5. To eat, and to drink, and to be merry.
6. Cast thy bread upon the waters; for thou shalt find it after many days.
7. Rejoice, O young man, in thy youth.

## PROVERBS

1. Go to the ant, thou sluggard; consider her ways and be wise.
2. Stolen waters are sweet, and bread eaten in secret is pleasant.
3. A wise son maketh a glad father.
4. In the multitude of counselors there is safety.
5. As a jewel of gold in a swine's snout, so is a fair woman which is without discretion.
6. The way of the transgressor is hard.
7. He that spareth his rod hateth his son.
8. A soft answer turneth away wrath.
9. Better is a dinner of herbs where love is than a stalled ox and hatred therewith.
10. Pride goeth before destruction, and a haughty spirit before a fall.
11. He that is slow to anger is better than the mighty; and he that ruleth his spirit than he that taketh a city.
12. He that repeateth a matter separateth friends.
13. A merry heart doeth good like a medicine.
14. Even a fool, when he holdeth his peace, is counted wise.
15. Whoso findeth a wife findeth a good thing.
16. Meddle not with him that flattereth with his lips.
17. It is better to dwell in a corner of the housetop than with a brawling woman in a wide house.
18. A good name is rather to be chosen than great riches.
19. Train up a child in the way he should go; and when he is old, he will not depart from it.
20. The borrower is servant to the lender.
21. Seest thou a man diligent in his business? He shall stand before kings.
22. As he thinketh in his heart, so is he.
23. Despise not thy mother when she is old.
24. A word fitly spoken is like apples of gold in pictures of silver.
25. Heap coals of fire upon his head.
26. Boast not thyself of tomorrow, for thou knowest not what a day may bring forth.
27. Better is a neighbor that is near than a brother far off.
28. A continual dropping in a very rainy day and a contentious woman are alike.

29. He that maketh haste to be rich shall not be innocent.
30. There be three things which are too wonderful for me, yea four which I know not: the way of an eagle in the air; the way of a serpent upon a rock; the way of a ship in the midst of the sea; and the way of a man with a maid.

## PSALMS

1. Out of the mouth of babes and sucklings.
2. What is man that thou art mindful of him? Yet has Thou made him but little lower than the angels.
3. He maketh me to lie down in green pastures; he leadeth me beside the still waters.
4. The valley of the shadow of death.
5. Thy rod and Thy staff, they comfort me.
6. My cup runneth over.
7. Keep my tongue from evil and my lips from speaking guile.
8. Blessed is he that considereth the poor.
9. God is our refuge and strength, a very present help in trouble.
10. The words of his mouth were smoother than butter, but war was in his heart.
11. Thou renderest to every man according to his work.
12. He went through fire and through water.
13. A day in Thy courts is better than a thousand. I had rather be a doorkeeper in the house of my God than to dwell in the tents of wickedness.
14. So teach us to number our days that we may apply our hearts unto wisdom.
15. As for man, his days are as grass; as a flower of the field, so he flourisheth.
16. Man goeth forth unto his work and to his labor until the evening.
17. They that sow in tears shall reap in joy.
18. Except the Lord build the house, they labor in vain that build it.
19. If I forget thee, O Jerusalem, let my right hand forget her cunning.

## JOB

1. The Lord gave and the Lord hath taken away; blessed be the name of the Lord.
2. Man is born unto trouble, as the sparks fly upward.
3. Speak to the earth, and it shall teach thee.
4. Man that is born of woman is of few days and full of trouble.
5. If a man die, shall he live again?
6. I am escaped with the skin of my teeth.
7. The price of wisdom is above rubies.
8. Great men are not always wise.
9. He multiplieth words without knowledge.

## CHRONICLES

1. Our days on the earth are as a shadow.

## KINGS

1. A wise and an understanding heart.
2. He (Solomon) spake three thousand proverbs; and his songs were a thousand and five.

3. A still, small voice.
4. Like the driving of Jehu, the son of Nimshi; for he driveth furiously.
5. Jezebel heard of it, and she painted her face and attired her head, and looked out at a window.
6. Set thine house in order.

## SAMUEL

1. Speak, Lord; for thy servant heareth.
2. And all the people shouted and said, "God save the king."
3. A man after his own heart.
4. So David prevailed over the Philistine with a sling and with a stone.
5. How are the mighty fallen!

## RUTH

1. Whither thou goest, I will go; and where thou lodgest, I will lodge; thy people shall be my people, and thy God my God.

## JUDGES

1. And Delilah said to Samson, Tell me, I pray thee, wherein thy great strength lieth.

## DEUTERONOMY

1. Man doth not live by bread alone.
2. The poor shall never cease out of the land.

## LEVITICUS

1. The swine is unclean to you. Of their flesh shall ye not eat.
2. Thou shalt love thy neighbor as thyself.
3. The Lord bless thee and keep thee; the Lord make his face shine upon thee and be gracious unto thee; the Lord lift up his countenance unto thee and give thee peace.

## EXODUS

1. A land flowing with milk and honey.
2. Honor thy father and thy mother.
3. Eye for eye, tooth for tooth, hand for hand, foot for foot.

## GENESIS

1. And God said, Let there be light; and there was light.
2. In the sweat of thy face shalt thou eat bread.
3. For dust thou art, and unto dust shalt thou return.
4. Am I my brother's keeper?
5. And the Lord set a mark upon Cain.
6. His (Ishmael's) hand will be against every man, and every man's hand against him.
7. His (Lot's) wife looked back from behind him, and she became a pillar of salt.

8. He (Jacob) dreamed, and behold a ladder set up on the earth, and the top of it reached to heaven; and behold the angels of the Lord ascending and descending it.
9. Mizpah - The Lord watch between me and thee, when we are absent one from the other.